What people are saying about *Zero to 100*

Endorsements of this book were NOT paid for. They were written on the value and merit of the content in this book.

I wish I had, had all of the insight and inspiration contained in Zero to 100™ when I first started out in my career. As an introvert who struggled with networking for many years and just recently found some rhythm and joy in the art of building REAL-ATIONSHIPS, Zero to 100™ was insightful and inspirational. The content, stories, and data all contribute to a holistic and people-centered approach to life and doing business that has the potential to be a life-changer in any industry and community. I especially like the tie-in to the personality assessments and using them to leverage your networking efforts.

– Gabriela Ramírez-Arellano, Business Strategist , Author

It seems that most individuals don't know how to effectively network, which often leads to frustration. As avid networkers and executive board members of a women's networking group that focuses on collaboration over competition, it's breathtaking that the Zero to 100 system echo's and validates this philosophy, while showing exactly how to build real relationships. Zero to 100 provides insights and strategies on how to effectively master the art of networking in the most sincere and meaningful way. Most impressive is the combined data of many individuals who have successfully executed these proven techniques with mind-blowing results. Once you read it and implement the methods described, your results will speak volumes and your frustration will turn into refreshing excitement! Zero to 100 will revolutionize the world of networking!

– Michell Stockmann, CEO Women Empowering Women
– Heather J. Crider, CSO Women Empowering Women

The research and work Mr. Joseph Luckett has put into Zero to 100 is the equivalent of having a coach right next to you at all times. When the principles found in this book are put into practice, it's like a written guarantee that you're word of mouth advertising will prove wildly successful!

Rich DeForest, Founder, NTi
(Networking Today International)

"Joseph is truly an expert at his craft. He taught me great skills needed for the business world – to be upbeat and passionate about what I do! He taught me how to network with business professionals and seek potential opportunities. He also helped me believe that I can grow my business through networking and by being an expert. I really enjoy his energetic and positive attitude!"

– Brian Schwabe, Account Manager at Gold Biotechnology, Inc.

"Joseph has helped me tremendously. He has introduced me to others who have helped me in my line of work. He is an awesome person who has a wealth of info to share and does so selflessly. His networking skills are very instrumental and much needed in this industry of sales and team building. Thank you, Joseph, for all that you do and have done personally for me, and always with a smile!"

– Frederica James, Credit Consultant at FES

"Joseph is a great friend and a great leader. His unique blend of extreme drive and integrity make him a role model and inspiration in the workplace. Joseph pursues excellence and aspires to greater character and competence every day. Joseph is also a generous giver, a professional whose connections benefit immensely from being a part of his network"

– Tony Holt, Business Coach, Faith, Fire, and Focus Coaching

The Gold Standard of Global Networking

JOSEPH LUCKETT

Zero to 100 Press

Zero to 100
The Gold Standard of Global Networking
Joseph Luckett
Zero to 100 Press

Published by Zero to 100 Press, St. Charles, MO

Content Writer: Anya Overmann, anyaovermann.com

Editors: Kristin D. Sadler, "Pen & Peacock Professional Writing" and Anya Overman, anyaovermann.com

Cover and Illustrations: Made You Look by K. Sonderegger

Project Management and Interior Design: Davis Creative Publishing Partners, DavisCreative.com

Publisher's Cataloging-In-Publication Data
(Prepared by The Donohue Group, Inc.)

Names: Luckett, Joseph, 1984- author.

Title: Zero to 100 : the gold standard of global networking / Joseph Luckett.

Description: St. Charles, MO : Zero to 100 Press, [2021] | The trademark symbol (™) appears immediately after Zero to 100 throughout this work.

Identifiers: ISBN 9781736677308 (paperback) | ISBN 9781736677315 (hardback) | ISBN 9781736677322 (ebook)

Subjects: LCSH: Business networks. | Interpersonal relations. | Business communication. | Social networks. | BISAC: SELF-HELP / Communication & Social Skills. | BUSINESS & ECONOMICS / Entrepreneurship. | BUSINESS & ECONOMICS / Business Etiquette.

Classification: LCC HD69.S8 L83 2021 (print) | LCC HD69.S8 (ebook) | DDC 650.1/3--dc23

Dedication

I first want to dedicate this book to coffee. Throughout this book, I draw many metaphors between networking and coffee. I understand that not everyone likes coffee, but for me, it holds an incredibly strong symbolism. So to fully appreciate the contents of this book, I want you to know what coffee means to me. For me, working for a coffee network marketing business opened doors and showed me I was capable of so much more – not just making more money, but more self-development and more potential to form connections. Aside from my appreciation of the beverage, a distant mentor once showed me the greater importance of coffee to humanity; it has the power to bring people together during both great and catastrophic times. Coffee crosses borders, languages, cultures, ethnicities, genders, and income brackets. Coffee does not discriminate. It is woven into the social fabrics of life and is a part of networking all over the world. Coffee helps to create the most important thing: relationships – or as you will see me refer to it in this book, "REAL-ationships." So not only did coffee help shape who I am today, but its symbolism drives a potential for shaping human connection. It is with that signifi-cance that I approach my networking philosophies, metaphors, and language in this book. Whether you like coffee or not, my hope is that you can appreciate where I'm coming from with coffee.

I dedicate this book to my parents, Harriet and James Luckett, and my entire family. My parents adopted me as an infant and immediately accepted me with love. Dad always made my dreams come true and Mom always had a surprise up her sleeve that would make me giddy. Whether it was a special holiday or a special meal, my parents made everything with love.

James and Harriet Luckett

Lastly, I dedicate this book to my wife – the best cup of coffee in my life, Carol Lynn Hinkle Luckett. She came up with the title of this movement – Zero to 100™. She helped me lay the ground-work for my creativity to scale this venture in ways only God could understand. My cup of coffee inspires me every day to become a better networker and connector, and without her, I would not have been able to grow from Zero to 100™ – not just in business, but also in my personal life.

Without these important people in my life, I would not be where I am today. I am forever grateful.

The key to successful networking is developing REAL-ationships— which is easier said than done if you don't have a plan.

Acknowledgments

I have been networking since July 15, 2011, and have so many people to thank for the impact they've had on me through networking – too many people to thank here. I thank all of you globally but also want to recognize some specific people who have helped me arrive where I am today.

Thank you to each of my educational institutions for giving me such wonderful teachers and experiences, Kindergarten through 12th grade. I owe education for lighting my incredible fire of inspiration. Not just the teachers, but the janitors, lunch ladies, librarians, special education teachers, principals, and the coaches who have all shaped me in ways for which I am forever grateful.

Thank you to the members of my Zero to 100™ Advisory Board. Without your tireless dedication, the contribution of time, a vast range of skills and knowledge, and motivation and drive to make Zero to 100™ a reality, my dream and this mission might never have taken on the life-changing scope that has emerged. Carol and I are eternally grateful and look forward to a lifetime of making networking better for everyone.

Thank you to Ron Ameln and the staff at the St. Louis Small Business Monthly for recognizing and promoting my work helping others and selecting me as one of "The Top 100 St. Louisans You Should Know to Succeed in Business." This is beyond an honor and I am forever grateful!

Thank you to the people who have inspired me:

Art Snarzyk, Sulaiman Rahman, Katie Grassi, Dan Main, Ann Carden, Michael Burke, Lori Ladd, Richard Billings, Holton Buggs,

DeMarcus Tunstall, Linah Elnashar, John U. Higgins, Gary Vaynerchuk, and many more.

I want to thank my #GrammarPatrol, who have significantly helped me with the language I use:

Anna Alt, Ruth Gerchen, Stephanie Berk, Matt D'Rion, Shary Raspy.

Thank you, Jeanne Hamra and Art Snarzyk, for spending hours deepening my understanding of DISC, Motivators, and Driving Forces and for presenting it as an asset to the Zero to 100™ community. You both have been instrumental in the writing of the DISC and Motivator information included in this book.

Thank you, Daniel Schmidt, for taking time away from your role as a Senior Research Project Manager at Pennsylvania State University, in the Edna Bennett Pierce Prevention Research Center, to conduct valuable research that lends more credibility and substance to the scientifically supported processes in the Zero to 100™ movement.

You must write a book with your process in it, and leave everyone with a piece of you. If you don't you would be doing everyone an injustice. Thank you so much, Laura Boedges, for believing in me. For that, I'm forever grateful to you!

Lastly, I want to offer a HUGE thanks to each person in networking who gave me the opportunity to meet with you. Without all those meetings that have led to REAL-ationships, Zero to 100™ wouldn't have been possible.

I have many more people to acknowledge, but now it's time to get into the heart of Zero to 100™. You can find the rest of these acknowledgments at the end of this book.

Table of Contents

Results of the Zero to 100™ Data Study: Social, Professional, Financial Improvements

In business, as in other areas, there are many ideas and myths that people promote as being 120% effective and true. However, without seeing the results of a study of the idea in real-world situations, how can business owners know what to listen to? It is with this in mind that we tested the principles that you will read about in this book.

We asked 38 business owners, salespeople, and consultants (both new and seasoned networkers from a variety of professions, backgrounds, and ethnicities) to read this book and implement what they read, keeping a weekly log of how much of the book they read, how closely they were following the principles in the book, and how the benefits and challenges of networking changed over a time period of 12 weeks. We then asked Daniel Schmidt, a researcher at Pennsylvania State University, to help us with the statistical results and conclusions.

The strategies and principles that are in this book were treated like hypotheses, which were put through a 12-week study starting on June 24, 2019, in real-life to better understand the effect they have on the networking and business practices of readers.[1] This study included a pre-test with multiple iterations of post-tests and identified significant improvements in the networking and business practices of those involved in the study. The results of the study are included in certain chapters throughout the book, as well as here at the beginning.

As you begin reading Zero to 100™, please keep in mind that the most important takeaway from the study was that **the benefits gained from this book are based on how closely you follow the principles of the book**. The benefits gained are *not* based on how much of the book you have read, *nor* how much time you dedicate to networking or maintaining your network. Simply put, the more closely you follow the principles of the book, the better your results from networking will be.

Correlation

	Challenges	Benefits
In the past week, how closely have you followed the principles of networking in Zero to 100?	.438**	.460**

Throughout the study, you will see references to "Challenges" and "Benefits." The term "Challenges" is a broad reference to specific networking challenges, which include: Starting Conversations, Ending Conversations, Building Rapport, Maintaining Relationships, Finding Reciprocal Relationships, Time Investment, and Financial Investment. The term "Benefits" is a broad reference to specific networking benefits, which include: Leads, Income, Job Opportunities, Creativity/Perspective, Professional Knowledge, and Friendships.

Participants of the study identified significant improvements to the benefits they received from networking when they followed the principles in this book. They had a decrease in the challenges they experienced during networking consistently through the period of research. More directly, the statistical analysis identified the following:

- 19.1% of the improvement to challenges shown in the graph were highly correlated with how closely respondents followed the principles in the book.
- 16% of the improved benefits shown in the graph were highly correlated with how closely respondents followed the principles in this book.

Many people understand the benefits of networking. As the old saying goes, "it's not what you know, it's *who* you know." Participants of the study indicated support of this adage and consistently identified improvements in every area that can be benefited by networking.

In areas of social development:

- Professional Advice/Support showed a 357% increase.
- Friendships showed a 328% increase.
- Personal Advice/Support showed a 317% increase.

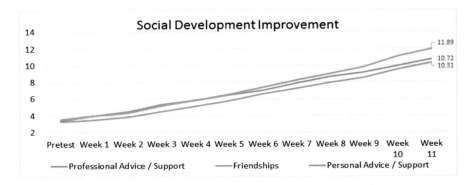

In areas of professional development:
- Creativity/Perspective showed a 391% increase.
- Professional knowledge showed a 344% increase.
- Career Advancement showed a 234% increase.

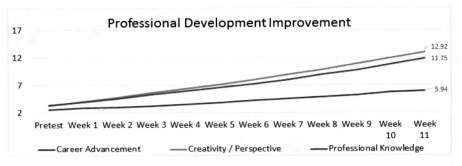

In areas of financial improvement:
- Leads showed a 279% increase.
- Job Opportunities showed a 212% increase.
- Income showed a 170% increase.

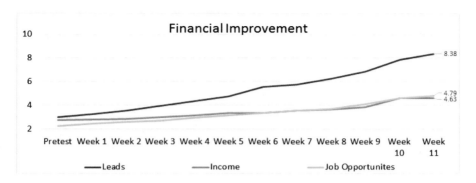

We are excited to bring you Zero to 100™, which is supported by statistics, and a real-world trial. If you simply follow the process and genuinely work to improve others' lives, it comes back to you in social, professional, and financial spades.

"Folks, get your hearts ready! Zero to 100™ is setting the Gold Standard in Global Networking. The statistical data conclusively proves that the Zero to 100™ process works. It is one of the FIRST (if not the only) networking books with a process supported by real-life data!"

– Zero to 100™ Board Member

Pay It "Foreword"

by Zach Tucker

I have a question for you. Yes, you — eager networker with this book in your hand. In your lifetime, do you believe you will change the world? Whether you're new to the world of networking, or you're a seasoned veteran of the coffee shop, I want you to really think about this. Sit back in your chair, close your eyes, open your Headspace® app and meditate if you have to … just think.

It's a big idea, right? What would you have to do to change the world? How many pairs of TOMS® would you have to buy? How many times would you have to give in and donate that $1 at the Walgreens register to TRULY change the world?

Now, be honest. Was your answer NO to believing you will change the world? "No, thanks! I've got a mortgage and four kids. I'll leave changing the world to those crazy Millennials." Or was your answer MAYBE? "Maybe, if I get off my butt and go on that mission trip with my church this year. Or, maybe when I retire, I'll start that nonprofit I've always thought about." Or perhaps, your answer is actually YES? "Yes, I've seen every Marvel movie 36 times and I already have my superhero costume designed in Canva!"

Whatever your answer happens to be, what if I told you that after reading this book about "networking," not only will you believe you can change the world, but you'll even have a step-by-step process on how to make it happen? Well, call me crazy if you want, but it's true.

For those of you who don't know who I am, I'm Zach Tucker — or as people in my network affectionately call me, Give Back Zach. Like many of you reading this book, I left my paycheck behind to take a ride on the entrepreneur roller coaster. Shortly after launching my first business in college, I was incredibly blessed to work around the world, land on the Inc. 500 and St. Louis 30 under 30 lists, and even receive an invitation to the White House. But in 2016, everything changed when I had my "ah-ha" moment and found my true passion in life-giving back, helping others, and making a difference in the world. Soon after this discovery, I launched a social impact startup with a mission to help businesses give back and support causes they held close to their hearts. After helping donate over $150,000 to our charity partners through the generosity of small business owners just like you, my wife and I sold this company in 2019. And that brings us to today, where I'm just another warrior in the nonprofit world working day and night to make our world a better place.

With all of that said, I'm not a professional networker, I'm not some startup bigshot, and no, I'm not famous. So why did THE Joseph Luckett ask some guy obsessed with changing the world to write the foreword to his book? It's an excellent question and it's also the first thing I asked him when he presented this opportunity. In classic Joseph fashion, he answered with a simple and wide-eyed, "Zach, just trust me."

Shortly after opening this book, the reasoning behind my involvement quickly became clear. The pages to follow aren't a guide to networking. Don't get me wrong — after reading this book you'll know EVERYTHING you need to become a ROCK STAR networker. But the heart, soul, and passion fire that burns within each line is actually a step-by-step guide to HELPING OTHERS.

As many of you know, Joseph has amassed a passionate following in the networking industry like no other. He's accomplished this by doing one simple thing ... putting other people's needs before his own. If you have ever had the honor of networking over a cup of coffee with Mr. Luckett, you don't leave the meeting with a list of ten people he wants to be connected to – you leave with ten introductions to people YOU want to be connected to. He places your needs before his own, and that's the secret sauce that has made Joseph so incredibly successful at networking. It also happens to be where this whole "change the world" concept I mentioned before comes into play.

Changing the world isn't what we've been brought up to think. Creating change doesn't have to be starting a nonprofit or moonlighting as a superhero. And you don't have to be a billionaire or a British rock star. Real, sustainable change happens when people, just like you and me, make daily efforts to help the people in our own lives (and our networks). It's really quite simple. Each time you make a difference in someone's life, a ripple effect begins. That life impacts another, which impacts another, and another, and so on ... this ripple is what truly changes the world.

As networkers, we all have the rare opportunity to ignite this change over a simple cup of coffee, almost daily. We all know what that crucial connection can do for our business. Whether it's a warm referral to that dream customer you've been chasing for months or an intro to a game-changer like Joseph, each connection can make a profound difference in the life of the recipient. In the following pages, you'll discover how to become a person who makes that difference by living in the mindset of helping others FIRST. If you follow the steps and techniques outlined ahead, not only will your networking get a whole lot better, but the world will as well.

I encourage you to not just read this book but to live it. Don't just network, help others. Don't just get coffee, change the world.

This Book Gives Back

The Zero to 100™ team's impact doesn't end at the coffee table. When I sat down with Joseph to discuss this book, the first thing he said to me was "Zach, I want this book to do more than help the readers...I want it to help people in need as well." From that moment on, Joseph and I set out to find a mission that aligned with the impact of the book. Like Zero to 100™ itself, it needed to be remarkable, unique, and larger than life. It didn't take us long to find that very mission, because one came to light and strongly fit the bill.

Every copy of Zero to 100™ sold supports Spirit of Discovery Park – a full-scale amusement park being developed in St. Louis, Missouri, specifically designed for children and individuals of ALL abilities.

Remember going to theme parks when you were younger? The rides, the food, the laughs, the excitement? To many of us, those are memories we will cherish for the rest of our lives. Unfortunately, there are children, parents, grandparents, and entire families across the world who have challenges preventing them from enjoying these experiences. Once built, these families will travel from destinations near and far to visit Spirit of Discovery Park, without the fear of a loved one missing out on the fun. By purchasing, reading, and spreading the word about Zero to 100™, you're part of building this beacon of hope that will impact lives for years to come.

Let's change the world together, friends.

Live INSPIRED,

Zach Tucker (a.k.a. Give Back Zach)
You can follow my giving journey at www.givebackzach.com.
To learn more about the Spirit of Discovery Park and support its mission, please visit www.spiritofdiscoverypark.com. Every dollar helps!

Preface

Are you a small business owner, sales professional, entrepreneur, or independent contractor looking for a better way to network? Additionally, if you are the owner or president of a networking group, this book will benefit your membership by cultivating the right culture and practices within your organization. Why? Because there is currently no one standard in networking – Zero to 100™ focuses on a universal networking process that works across cultures, communities, and industries. After incorporating our principles into your networking routine, you will see how we are setting a gold standard that truly helps establish bridges. Regardless of whether your group is membership-based or not, this book will support attendance and retention while providing expectations and guidance to those who are new to building their business through networking.

Over the years, I've met with many people who have successfully applied the Zero to 100™ networking principles all over the world. Dozens upon dozens have put testimonials on social media about how applying these philosophies has dramatically changed their businesses. Whether it's as simple as learning how to give an effective email introduction or as deep as shifting to a more giving mindset in networking, the Zero to 100™ principles have created a huge impact.

Instead of just taking my word for it, the Zero to 100™ content that you are about to read is supported and validated by data. The principles in this book have been treated as hypotheses and put through a study that now statistically support the efficiency and effectiveness of the process with participants from across the United States covering different ethnicities, races, and generations.

- Gen Z, iGen, or Centennials: Born 1996 – TBD
- Millennials or Gen Y: Born 1977 – 1995
- Generation X: Born 1965 – 1976
- Baby Boomers: Born 1946 – 1964
- Traditionalists or Silent Generation: Born 1945 and before

The research study graphs and tables throughout the book are credited to Daniel Schmidt who led, ran, and conducted our study. He conducted this study separately from his role as a Senior Research Project Manager at Pennsylvania State University.

This book is designed to give business owners and sales professionals an exact blueprint to systematically and comfortably work through each step of networking to gain consistent referral partners and grow each others' businesses. I also share honest pitfalls to be aware of so you can become a more effective networker and/or connector. My goal is to show you how to go from Zero to 100™ with a proven blueprint – from not being on anyone's radar to being on everyone's radar, whether they realize it or not. Once you read this book, I look forward to hearing about the amazing success and growth stories from each of you. Welcome to your future ...

"your networking just got a whole lot better!"

To pre-register for the Zero to 100™ Platform and get updates about news and events, visit this link: https://zeroto100.io/

This mosaic of photos includes 100 different networkers with whom I've connected in St. Louis

Planting the Coffee Seed

Who is Joseph Luckett?

Coffee begins as a green seed that's planted and grown into a coffee tree. Similarly, growth in networking starts with the seed you plant — that seed is who you are. I feel it's important for you to get to know me, my journey, and my motivation for Zero to 100™. This will give you an idea of how my coffee seed grew into a coffee tree, and maybe inspire you to contemplate how you're growing and changing to become the best version of yourself too. Happy reading!

Hello, I'm Joseph Luckett

I've always been ambitious, wired a little differently, and some have called me a dreamer. However, everything I do is intentional and purpose-driven, because if you leave your life to chance, then a chance life is all you will have.

As a kid, I was known as "Joey." *"Keep your focus on the task, Joey." "Eyes up front, Joey." "Joey, stop talking."* These are just a few of the reprimands I heard often from my teachers and parents. Some might call it Attention Deficit Disorder (ADD) or hyperactive, I now know it as *me*.

Growing up I was a very determined kid and I loved video games. I would stay up all night long trying to defeat the next level and the game itself. You would always find me in front of the TV jumping up and down, tongue hanging out of my mouth, relentless until I won. That trait of determination carried into my physical goals too – I taught myself how to breakdance and how to tumble by watching videos.

"Once he has his mind made up, he doesn't change it until he succeeds or fails. That's what I love about him the most."

– Rod, nephew

Breakdancing was one of the most challenging physical hobbies in my life because it took months to get just one move, then connecting the moves took a few more months, and mastering the technique took another few months. But I was obsessed and focused. Craig, my buddy in high school, worked with me at breakdancing and we ended up performing in the school talent show. Our famous coordinated back-tucks on stage at St. Charles West High School not only won us the talent show but inspired other classmates to learn to breakdance.

Breakdancing Performance with Craig at the
St. Charles West High School Talent Show in 2001/02.

I began teaching people how to breakdance and we practiced in open gyms and in the grass. On Sunday nights, the former country line-dance club called Incahoots turned into a place for break-dancing circles with my buddies. Many of my breakdancing friends went on to be successful, worldwide dancers. I ended up teaching my youngest brother, Marlon, how to breakdance too. Now he's an incredible tumbler who can throw difficult skills like double-fronts and double-fulls — all from learning on the grass in our backyard.

Breakdancing April 12, 2018, in the RaisingSails Marketing entryway.

The intensity with which I study, practice, and master a subject I find interesting is something that has remained consis-tent throughout my life. Whether it's breakdancing or networking, my process remains the same — observe, absorb, compartmentalize, and teach it to someone else. Learning is a continual process and it's how I've come to achieve whatever I have sought.

"I used to tell his mother, Harriet, that one day he was gonna be a billionaire and she would laugh. I'd say 'no, for real, he's gonna be a billionaire.' And by God, he's on his way."

— Kaye Wilson, family

It doesn't make sense to talk about how I've become who I am today without explaining where I came from. I believe the formative years of childhood give us the core of who we become and it's up to our parents and the village of people who raise us to help develop the God-given gift that lies within each of us.

God placed me in the company of great people all the way back to when I was a baby. I received the gift of a family the day I was placed in the home of Harriet and James Luckett. They took me in as a foster child several days after my birth and decided that with my "peaceful" demeanor they wanted to move forward and adopt me. Little did they know, once I learned the power of my voice, there was no stopping me! And it's a good thing too because I quickly became one of seventeen children. It's a well-known fact that my parents were saints. My father was a hardworking man who enjoyed an ice-cold beer from time-to-time and quiet drives to Troy, Missouri, where he grew up, to visit friends and family. My mother was the matriarch of not only our home but also our church and community. Everyone knew of Miss Harriet! Our home was always buzzing with people from aunts to cousins, to older siblings stopping by to see what Mom cooked that day, to a simple knock on the door from a neighbor.

I was in the middle of my siblings in age, so not only did I have siblings close to my age dealing with the same pubescent issues, I had an older sibling group that kept us in line and were basically an extension of my parents when us younger kids messed up. Being one of seventeen siblings, this dynamic was much-needed. My parents had an enormous passion for children and helping the less fortunate. They never could stand to see a child suffer and would always provide an open door for family, neighbors, and the foster system when a child needed stability and love. This household environment helped everyone who came into our family, whether they were there for ninety days or a lifetime. This giving environment developed us into adults who truly understand the value of having a village participate in the upbringing of a child. We were (and still are!) the lucky ones because our village consisted of family.

I'm asked almost daily, "Joseph, how did you get to be the way you are now?" I'm asked what I listen to or read to develop my level of focus, patience, and understanding of people. The truth is, I haven't read anything different than most entrepreneurs. I now believe, thanks to my wife Carol, that most of who I am is innate. Carol will attest that we complement each other well – while I'm driven to meet and get to know people, she is more introverted and doesn't enjoy networking. She is slower to trust than I am, which brings harmony to our relationship and we make a great team because of it.

I believe we are all given a set of gifts that are either developed throughout childhood or wasted from lack of use. I feel so blessed that I could freely develop those gifts without any reservation. I was free to be creative in all aspects of my life, from the way I wanted to dress to the music I wanted to listen to. We had discipline with love, and responsibility with understanding, much of which is lost today inside the world of technology and parents working extra-long hours without much time for family. Our days were full of weed pulling, family time at the park, and a house overflowing with food and friends. Many of the children my parents helped along the way continued to visit our home and attend family events until my parents passed away in 2012.

When it comes to my business experience, I can honestly say that I have not had many jobs. From my first job as a cashier and fry guy at Arby's to my last job as a computer sales associate at Best Buy, my experience working for someone else has been short-lived. That's a good thing. I discovered early on that working for someone is just not in my DNA. My personality is the kind that needs the freedom to say and do and what works best for me in order to be successful. Finding a way to fiddle through company scripts and properly canned spiels to get the needed response did not work for me. There's an old song by Sammy Davis Jr. called, "I Gotta Be Free." The first verse ends with, "I gotta be me, I've gotta be me. What else can I be but what I am?" Well, when I first heard it, I thought that pretty well sums me up — and so my quest to find my own way began.

When I worked as a telemarketer, I was introduced to an industry where I could be my own boss. I remember it vividly — it was November 11, 2006. I'd been invited to a high-energy network marketing meeting in a hotel in St. Charles, Missouri. The only words I took away that night were this: for every three people who decided to do this with me, I would earn $311. Hmm, that easy? At only 22 years old, that was a lot of money to me. I thought about all the friends who went to college with me who had a lot of friends who went to college with them, and so on. We could all do quite well with this!

At the following week's meeting, I had 15 friends join me. The next week, I had 17 guests and they all joined. Do you catch my drift? I found a way to earn money exponentially and without a boss. This was like owning my own business and it was my introduction to becoming an entrepreneur — and I loved it! We were being exposed to the power of self-development where each week a speaker with a book shared their story. All I wanted to do was to read, read, read. I became a sponge; the knowledge that filled my brain was so overwhelming, I had to share it so I could fill it up with more.

I spent the next five years working for various network marketing companies. First, I sold legal services where I made $36,000 in the first six months. I didn't know it was possible to make six figures a year without a full-time job. Then I switched to another network marketing company, which turned out to be a terrible experience but I learned a lot. The person who sponsored me was deceptive and greedy, and the company ultimately went under because people were embezzling. That's when I moved to another network marketing company in the health industry where I made $1200 each week on autopilot while working full time at Best Buy. This company also ended up going under due to mismanaged growth.

Then in June 2010, I was asked to look into a company named Organo Gold (now Organo[2]). This is where I ultimately found success in network marketing and when coffee became a significant part of my life. My mentor at Organo was making a million dollars every twenty days, which I never knew was possible. That's fifty cents every second! This is who taught me the philosophies that I apply to Zero to 100™ and my networking process. He also taught me the important role coffee plays in our lives. Sixty-four percent of Americans drink a cup of coffee every day. Coffee plants are cultivated in more than 70 countries and it is one of the most popular drinks in the world. So much business is conducted around the world over a cup of coffee, it is the reason why the beverage ties into so many Zero to 100™ metaphors: **coffee is networking.**

Just shy of a year with Organo, May 20th, 2011, was the last day I had a full-time, regular job. That's the day I quit Best Buy and became a full-time network marketer with Organo. I've been growing ever since.

My experiences in network marketing provided the knowledge to lay the foundation for my own networking practices. Network marketing makes you look at yourself in the mirror; **it's a self-reflective industry – it's not about how smart you are, it's about how good you are at putting people first. Entrepreneurship is self-reflective too. You have to work on yourself to be successful, and then fall in love with people. In both network marketing and networking, you are stripped down to your values, so your accountability to others is paramount.**

These are the ideals upon which I decided to build the Zero to 100™ Networking Platform. With no standard in the networking community, I've found multiple missing pieces to the networking model, such as:

- What questions to ask in networking
- How to successfully set up introductions
- Structured scheduling
- Calculating ROI (return on investment)
- How to learn the culture and mindset to form authentic relationships
- How to navigate virtual networking

With education and exposure, we can resolve the lack of information about networking organizations being readily available to nearly everyone in every community, and we can address the lack of diversity within those groups. There's a serious lack of people of color in the networking community; Zero to 100™ unifies all ethnicities simply through *authentic relationship building*. In fact, all networking is made more viable by building REAL relationships – or REAL-ationships, as I call them. With a structured platform and an app to help you network better with more accountability, there is now measurable data for the importance of networking with the right intent and the potential to create an enormous culture both online and offline.

In this book, we dive into my tried-and-tested networking process, which I've developed over thousands of meetings. This system caters to all personalities and people of all ethnicities, races, cultures, nationalities, genders, abilities, and backgrounds. Why? Because Zero to 100™ networking isn't about what *you* can get out of it – it's about genuinely connecting with others and finding ways to bring value into others' lives. It's about helping people find that hundredth connection in networking that up-levels their business because if you can *bring value to your connections*, you'll go from nobody knowing your name to everyone knowing your name. To find real success in networking, your network shouldn't just have people who look like you or act like you. Your network should bridge across industries, geographical regions, and cultures. When you seek to bring value to a diverse network, value comes back to you as a byproduct. Having a diverse network is not only beneficial to you and your business by opening up so many new opportunities, but these connections also help create bridges over prejudice. Effective networking is a process of reciprocity, and it starts with you and me.

Bringing it Back to Coffee

This – my story and my experience – is how I grew and harvested my coffee seed to ultimately become a hot cup of coffee in networking and how I came to develop the Zero to 100™ Networking Platform.

CHAPTER 1

Growing the Coffee Cherry

What is Networking?

Coffee trees grow cherries that contain coffee beans on the inside. That coffee bean must be grown, harvested, and processed to provide the best, hot cup of coffee possible. Like the cherry, we grow the fruit of who we are to form the coffee bean inside, or in this case, we grow personally and professionally to form real connections with others in networking until we get to the most reciprocal hot coffee meeting. In this chapter, you will learn what networking is and the core Zero to 100™ concepts that will grow your best coffee cherry and inner bean to connect with others.

You could stop reading here and still understand that the bottom line of the Zero to 100™ networking formula is about REAL-ationships. But if you do stop reading now, you'll miss out on how to develop those REAL-ationships for yourself and transform them into networking success.

My journey to understand networking began in June of 2010 when I was invited to a meeting by a friend who owned a cleaning company. This was a structured networking event (structured networking will be discussed in Chapter 2) with a set schedule of timed events over ninety minutes. I never knew something like this existed and it totally blew me away. When this group shared how much income they earned the week prior from one another's referrals, I began compartmentalizing how all of this worked. I pondered how I could fit into networking and bring even more value to people. I paid close attention to each person as they shared their success, but I was puzzled why some people had a ton of financial success while others didn't have much at all. After the meeting, the person who invited me pulled me aside to hear my thoughts. I said it was incredible and asked about attending the next one.

The funny thing about this new world I'd just been exposed to was that I thought it was just a thing that existed here in St. Charles, Missouri. I had no idea this was something I could do everywhere! This exposure to networking struck my curiosity, and as I always do when something piques my interest, I suddenly had a laser-focused intent to learn more. Everyone who knows me knows that I do not stop my inquiry until I truly understand something. Unfortunately, my initial experience with networking wasn't ideal because I didn't feel welcomed. I just couldn't understand why everyone wasn't as excited as I was – **your energy introduces you before you even open your mouth**. Your intentionality is so important. When I stepped up to the registration table at the event, there was nobody to greet me, and then I sat next to two people who didn't say a word to me. After that experience, I decided I never wanted anyone I network with to feel that way. Even if someone is uncertain and new, we as networkers should make it a point to welcome and reach out to everyone. One of my favorite quotes is "only go where you are celebrated, not where you are tolerated." I made it my mission to celebrate everyone I came in contact with – and so my networking adventure began, as did the basis for what I now call the Networking Formula to Success.

Networking Formula to Success

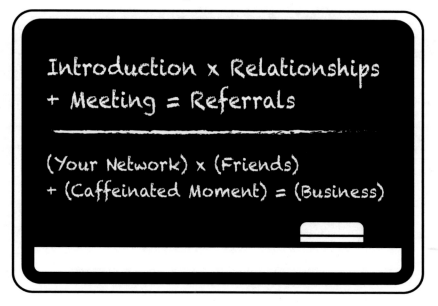

Introduction x Relationships
+ Meeting = Referrals
––––––––––––––––––––––
(Your Network) x (Friends)
+ (Caffeinated Moment) = (Business)

This formula is about getting to know people you like and trust so you can get the best referrals in business. **Referrals are connections to people who are already warmly interested in your product or service – people who are likely to feed your business revenue.** So that begs the question: how do you put together the other pieces of the formula to get more referrals? Let me break it down for you.

Introductions (Your Network)

This piece of the formula is your potential to know people in your network. **An introduction is when two people are introduced to one another through a friend or a mutual acquaintance**. There is an established level of trust where both parties are comfortable opening their network and bringing people to the table that can benefit each other's revenue line, network, or both.

Relationship or REAL-ationship (Friends and People You Trust)

This is about the depth of connection between you and another. The stronger the relationship, the stronger the potential for referrals in both directions.

Meeting (Caffeinated Moment)

This last piece of the formula is the actual work of building relationships. How do you get to know someone with the sole intent to learn about that person other than sitting down with him or her and listening? The meeting is the time investment in networking – the investment in REAL-ationships.

When I first started networking on July 15, 2011, I set goals that would astonish everyone, including myself, like scheduling 500 meetings in 90 days using the local coffee shops as my meeting ground. I knocked this first goal out of the park within 74 days. Then, 45 days later, I had scheduled another 500 meetings. So within 129 days, I had met with more than 1,000 people. In the process of these meetings, I created a tool to help me efficiently develop REAL-ationships in my meetings over coffee. The tool is the **Caffeinated Moment.** Remember, I said I love my coffee! I know not everyone loves coffee, but according to Reuters in 2018, 64% of Americans drink a cup of coffee everyday.[3]

I wanted a new and refreshing way to schedule meetings and learn about my new connections that would be universally understandable and make a lasting impression, so I created the Caffeinated Moment (see the following form). It is a comfortable ice breaker and makes it easier to make the most of your time together—be it face-to-face or in a virtual setting. After all, the meetings are meant to be productive and create a connection, or a REAL-ationship. So, next time you ask someone for a "one-to-one," change it up and ask for a "Caffeinated Moment!"

Like most networkers, I have a cup of coffee at many of my meetings. That coffee perks me up and leaves me refreshed, alert, and ready to go! This is exactly the kind of feeling I strive to leave each person I meet with – refreshed and ready to go!

Caffeinated Moment Form

Customize this form to your company/business and simplify the way you respond to a question like, "What does your company do?" It takes the nervousness out of the meeting with preparedness. You won't forget the important parts.

As you may already know, my company is _____**(name)** and we have/are _____**(background)**. My company offers _____**(product/service information)**. So, you know about _____**(competitor)**, right? Well, this is how we are **different**: _____. Our **market** is _____. We typically **deliver** to our market by _____.

Then give some **background** about your company:

- When the company began
- How many customers/end users/clients you have
- Number of employees and/or type
- Size of the company/how many locations
- Privately owned, incorporated, partnership, etc.

- Revenue information/debt-free (show profitability and success so they know it's reputable)
- Geography – where you conduct business
- Is your business an online model, offline model, or both? Does it have the capacity to run remotely?

(See the Appendix for more details about the Caffeinated Moment Form.)

Now that your new contact knows all about you and your company – specifically what and who you are looking for – you can explain to them how you want to be introduced to your market. You can share examples of how others properly introduce you. Offer to send an email with this filled-out Caffeinated Moment Form or a specific written example so it's easy for your new connection to edit it and refer you via email or in a text. Be sure this person knows it's okay to use the examples you provide. This will help them plug in your basic information and portray confidence when introducing you. And be sure to ask your new connection to send a completed Caffeinated Moment Form to you about themself as well. That way you can reciprocate.

Creating the best Caffeinated Moment during your initial encounter is the most effective way to leave a lasting impression. You want to make the most out of your meeting because you never know when you might meet this person again (hopefully, it's several times per year, even if you meet virtually). Perhaps when you do meet again, it will be when that person is in a different field or company – and since you were effective in building a personal rapport during your first meeting, all you need to know now is how to make a referral for this person's new profession. The more memorable the impression you leave with someone, the bigger the impact you can have on the networking community.

A Note About Virtual Networking

While I don't believe virtual networking is a long-term sustainable solution, it has become a necessity for staying connected in the wake of COVID-19. The benefit of virtual networking, other than helping us curb the effects of the 2020 pandemic, is that it can be more efficient than in-person networking. It cuts out travel time and allows for you to more easily stack meetings (more on the concept of Stack Days in Chapter 5). However, virtual networking is lacking in several ways: it requires a good internet connection and a functioning device, and there are far more variables out of your control as compared to in-person networking, where the environment is well-contained and distractions and interruptions are minimal. Networking exclusively through virtual means makes it harder to both develop and maintain relationships in the same capacity as face-to-face meetings. Ideally, virtual networking should be used as a supplemental effort to your in-person networking.

In our networking study each week, participants were asked, "As a result of reading Zero to 100™, please rate how each of the following challenges to networking has changed." As you can see, participants of the study showed significant improvements in many of the aspects of networking that most new networkers find especially challenging when they first begin networking. As with all participant improvements, the benefits directly correlated to how closely they followed the principles of the book.

CHAPTER 2

Harvesting the Coffee Cherry to Get the Best Bean

Using DISC & Motivators to Understand Networking

When harvesting the coffee cherry to reveal the bean inside, you learn what to look for with each cherry and bean, and you get a feel for whether each unique bean will go through the process to become a cup of coffee. In networking, when you understand your behavioral traits, the unique traits of others, and how you interact with those around you, you gain insight to adapt your communication style to best fit the conversation and personality of the connection you're meeting with. This develops your inner "coffee bean" and helps you move forward to the pinnacle of the process — a hot cup of coffee. I have found one of the best ways to do this is with DISC.

DISC is a behavior model based on the work of William Marston, Ph.D.[4] The DISC model addresses the way people respond to problems and challenges (D), people and contacts (I), pace and consistency (S), and procedures and constraints (C). Your specific DISC profile is a blend of the four behaviors. DISC alone is only one piece of the puzzle that makes up what is commonly referred to as your personality. Another crucial piece of the personality puzzle is what motivates you. The Six Motivators discussed here are based on the work of Eduard Spranger, Ph.D. His model addresses what drives or motivates people to do what they do. The motivators are the "why." The DISC behaviors are the "how."

While developing the Networking Formula to Success and applying the Caffeinated Moment, I was introduced to DISC through the organization TTI.[5] It was exciting to do my own DISC assessment to learn about my behaviors and motivators from a scientific standpoint and how this information could help me become a better communicator. What I immediately loved about DISC was the philosophy behind it: treat others the way *they* want to be treated, not the way *you* want to be treated.

To the extent that you give others what they want and need,
they will give you what you want and need.

The creators of the DISC and Motivator assessments understand that people are the number one product — the better you are with people, the more money you're going to make. I've researched many interpersonal communication models; none thoroughly explain behavioral styles in quite the same way nor do they offer the practical knowledge of *how* to communicate within each of them.

Each letter of DISC shows a measure of the behavioral attributes that, when combined, give the scope of your full presence. Taking the DISC assessment reveals where in each area of DISC you fall. It is important to note, the results will provide a blend of traits; they are not meant to say you are solely a High "D" or a Low "C," you will have behaviors from each of the four quadrants, as will your connections.

The following overview of DISC is meant to help you adapt in the networking environment, address your blind spots in relation to those you connect with, and make the most of your efforts when relating to varying types of personalities, just like it did for me. However, it's important to note that this tool is designed to help you observe and make sense of the different personalities you will encounter throughout in-person networking. Unfortunately, a lot of nuance is lost through virtual meetings and unless you are highly skilled at reading body language and know which questions to ask, it's very challenging to apply DISC in the same way. After this overview, I'll provide some questions you can ask in a virtual networking setting to make up for some of what's lost when networking through screens.

"D" is for Dominant and Direct

A person described as a High "D," or Dominant, would be assertive, results-oriented, and impatient. This is the type of person who, at a networking meeting, wears bold colors, looks you in the eye, gives you a solid nonverbal greeting (a firm handshake or perhaps an emphatic fist elbow bump), and gestures a lot when speaking. A Low "D" is the opposite – non-confrontational, submissive, and indecisive. This person, who is a lower "D," is more likely to be introverted and reserved in group networking situations, unless the Low "D" is paired with a High "I."

The High "D" is often the loudest person in the room, very assertive, quick to anger, and their focus on getting results rather than connecting with people may come across as the bull in a china shop.

Quick Facts – nationalities with "D" as their highest trait:
- 17% of Americans
- 17% of British
- 23% of Russians
- 11% of Chinese

"I" is for Influential and Interpersonal

A High "I," or Influential, behavior style is a people-person – outgoing, popular, and trusting. These people are fun and enjoyable to talk to because they're so personable. Low "Is," on the other hand, are not people-oriented and prefer to be more reserved at networking events. They're more cautious of trusting people and generally don't lead the conversation.

The High "I" is often thought of as a social butterfly, very chatty and expressive, and always looking for fun.

Quick Facts – nationalities with "I" as their highest trait:
- 38% of Americans
- 38% of Italians
- 40% of British
- 33% of Russians
- 33% of Dutch

"S" is for Steady and Stable

Someone who scores on the assessment as a High "S" is all about routine, consistency, and being methodical. In networking environments, steady, stable people dress simply and comfortably, make small gestures and subtle expressions, and they take their time opening up to people. A Low "S," on the other hand, is all about change and variety.

The High "S" is a supporter and a great listener. This person is reserved but friendly and warm, and feels very at-home in a quiet get-together with a few friends.

Quick Facts – nationalities with "S" as their highest trait:
- 32% of Americans
- 32% of Chinese
- 35% of Dutch
- 34% of French
- 34% of Australians
- 24% of Russians

"C" is for Conscientiousness and Correct

A High "C" is analytical, logical, and systematic. These are conscientious and correct people who wear conservative attire, are very reserved, and may avoid eye contact. High "Cs" are stereotypically CPAs or engineers – they are meticulous and want things to be precise. But a Low "C" doesn't care so much about accuracy and doesn't need as much information as a High "C" to make a decision.

The High "C" is less comfortable in social situations and would be more comfortable creating a spreadsheet than attending a party.

Quick Facts – nationalities with "C" as their highest trait:
- 13% of Americans
- 22% of Chinese
- 20% of Russians

Using Big Data to Better Appreciate Cultural Differences

Country	D	I	S	C
USA	17%	38%	32%	13%
Russia	23%	33%	24%	20%
China	11%	35%	32%	22%
Germany	19%	35%	33%	13%
Brazil	18%	36%	32%	14%
UK	17%	40%	29%	15%
Australia	18%	36%	34%	12%
Netherlands	21%	33%	35%	12%
France	18%	35%	34%	13%
Italy	19%	38%	30%	13%

© 2014 Target Training International   **Using Big Data to Better Appreciate Cultural Differences**

The ability to observe and identify DISC traits in the people you network with comes in handy when you start matching people up based on behaviors and values.

Even though we are all a blend of the four traits, you may be able to detect someone's dominant behavioral style(s) with the following two questions:

1. Extrovert or introvert?

   Extroverts get their energy from being with people and generally thrive in a group networking environment. Introverts get their energy from being by themselves and might withdraw at group networking events, however, they may open up in a Caffeinated Moment setting.

2. People or tasks?

   Folks who are people-oriented will talk about events, community, and other people. People who are task-oriented talk more about things like to-do items, activities, or research rather than people.

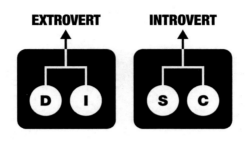

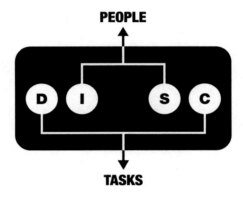

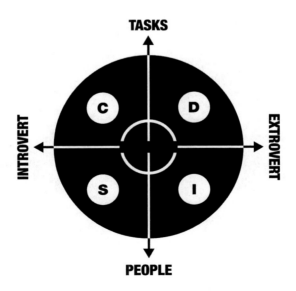

As mentioned, these DISC traits do not define who you are, nor does everyone fall into a clear-cut category. For example, there are extroverted introverts who love people but have to recharge by being alone. Some folks enjoy a mix of both people-oriented and task-oriented activities. The key to learning how someone might be identified in terms of DISC is to be present and observe their behaviors. And when in doubt, just ask a person how they'd describe themselves: extroverted or introverted? People- or task-oriented? In any case, this information is helpful to guide how you relate to each individual.

As promised earlier in the chapter, here are some questions that you can ask in a virtual meeting, whether it be on the phone or over a video call, to bring out a person's personality in a congruent way to how they show up in person.

1. How do you like to spend your free time?
2. What was your dream job growing up?
3. If you had a chance for a "do-over" in life, what would you do differently?
4. What teacher in school made the most impact on you and why?
5. What is the craziest, most outrageous thing you want to achieve?

You can find the full list of 20 questions to ask in a virtual setting in the Appendix.

It is essential to remember that one of the most important aspects of applying DISC to networking is learning to adapt your own behavior. Each behavior style has blind spots. Understanding your natural tendencies and blind spots gives you clues on how to adapt to others. For example, depending on your traits, the behaviors of a chatty "I" or an abrupt "D" could be more off-putting to an introverted "S" or "C." Learning to temper *your* behavior allows for better communication and for REAL-ationships to develop more easily.

Tip: As you get to know DISC and apply it, have a list of the key behavior descriptions on-hand when you meet with connections and write down their traits as you go through your Caffeinated Moment.

Now that you can see *how* people behave using DISC, you need to know what motivates them in life. Our motivators are our values – they're what get us excited and drive us to take action.

The Six Motivators, based on the work of Dr. Eduard Spranger in the early 20th century, offer insight on *why* we behave the way we do, which cannot be observed easily, they are learned by getting to know someone.

The Six Internal Motivators

1. Theoretical

The goal is to discover truth and knowledge. High theoreticals value education, research, and comprehension. They're excited to learn. A low theoretical person prefers to gain knowledge by instinct and experience rather than in-depth research. Examples of professions with a tendency toward the high theoretical motivator: professors, engineers, researchers, people with doctorates.

2. Utilitarian

The goal is practicality and good value. A high utilitarian is looking for the best return on their investment of resources and is generally resourceful. A low utilitarian finds value in the task-at-hand without concern for ROI. Examples of professions that lean toward the high utilitarian motivator: salespeople, business owners, financial advisors.

3. Aesthetic

The goal is harmony in surroundings and personal environment. A high aesthetic values experiences and enjoyable environments. A low aesthetic values function. Examples of professions that lean toward the high aesthetic motivator: interior decorators, architects, environmentalists.

4. Social

The goal is to eliminate hate and conflict. A high social is altruistic and driven to serve others for the sake of being helpful. A low social serves others when it is mutually beneficial or the person has a specific skill set that is needed. Examples of professions that lean toward the high social motivator: caregivers, therapists, nurses, people who work in nonprofits.

5. Individualistic

The goal is to assert oneself and gain prestige. A high individualistic seeks recognition and is competitive and commanding. A low individualistic values collaboration. Examples of professions with a tendency for high individualistic motives: politicians, celebrities, CEOs.

6. Traditional

The goal is to search for a system of living. A high traditional seeks belonging and something to believe in. This individual prefers a tried-and-true way of doing things. A low traditional is more receptive to new ways of doing things and likes to think outside the box. Examples of professions with a tendency toward the high traditional motivator: CFOs, law enforcement, people who work for faith-based businesses.

INSTINCTIVE	THEORETICAL	INTELLECTUAL
People who are driven by utilizing past experiences, intuition and seeking specific knowledge when necessary.	KNOWLEDGE	People who are driven by opportunities to learn, acquire knowledge and the discovery of truth.

SELFLESS	UTILITARIAN	RESOURCEFUL
People who are driven by completing tasks for the greater good, with little expectation of personal return.	UTILITY	People who are driven by practical results, maximizing both efficiency and returns for their investments of time, talent, energy and resources.

OBJECTIVE	AESTHETIC	HARMONIOUS
People who are driven by the functionality and objectivity of their surroundings.	SURROUNDINGS	People who are driven by the experience, subjective viewpoints and balance in their surroundings.

INTENTIONAL	SOCIAL	ALTRUISTIC
People who are driven to assist others for a specific purpose, not just for the sake of being helpful or supportive.	OTHERS	People who are driven by the benefits they provide others.

COLLABORATIVE	INDIVIDUALISTIC	COMMANDING
People who are driven by being in a supporting role and contributing with little need for individual recognition.	POWER	People who are driven by status, recognition and control over personal freedom.

RECEPTIVE	TRADITIONAL	STRUCTURED
People who are driven by new ideas, methods and opportunities that fall outside a defined system for living.	METHODOLOGIES	People who are driven by traditional approaches, proven methods and a defined system for living.

My friend Art Snarzyk is a Behavioral Analyst and DISC expert. He is a self-proclaimed introvert who has built an international consultancy through networking. He has learned several strategies, mindsets, and tools to make networking and connecting with others easier. He uses social sciences to help us all understand and accept ourselves and others, and to create a life we love without feeling like we have to "be someone else." Art introduced me to the concept of DISC, and true to my nature, I wanted to learn more.

It just so happens that one of my Zero to 100™ board members, Jeanne Hamra, is also a Certified Behavior/Driving Forces Analyst and DISC and Motivators expert. With her guidance, I took the assessment to learn how it might help me become a better networker. Once I was debriefed on my results, I was able to apply the information to deepen my understanding, fine-tune my application of the principles, and make better connections. Here is my DISC and Motivator profile:

Graph II

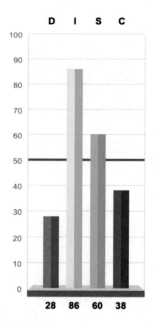

D = Dominant/Direct, I = Influential/Interpersonal,
S = Steady/Stable, C = Cautious/Correct

6 Inner Motivators

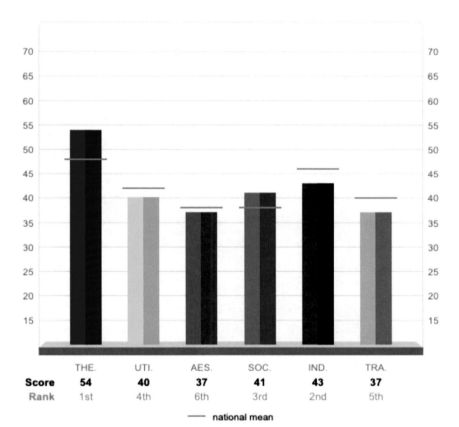

	THE.	UTI.	AES.	SOC.	IND.	TRA.
Score	**54**	**40**	**37**	**41**	**43**	**37**
Rank	1st	4th	6th	3rd	2nd	5th

——— national mean

THE. = Theoretical, UTI. = Utilitarian, AES. = Aesthetic,
SOC. = Social, IND. = Individualistic, TRA. = Traditional

When I learned that I'm a High "I"/Low "D" personality with strong Theoretical, Individualistic, and Social motivators, I immediately put together how I fit into the networking process. More importantly, I considered the type of value I could offer to everyone around me. First, I wanted to introduce those with whom I met to more people than they have ever met in their lives. Second, people often don't believe in who they are, which stifles business and personal growth, so I wanted to believe in everyone *more* than they believe in themselves. And third, I knew I would out-work everyone I met, lead by example, and set standards for how to get the most out of networking. I realized this was my chance to pioneer a space that no one had truly tapped into yet and decided to make this my ultimate goal.

Like every business owner, you want your customers to have a great experience with your product or service. My goal was no different when I started than it is today – to give everyone the best "Joseph Luckett" experience possible. I knew if I could effectively execute my goal, I would forever stay relevant. Because when you have a great experience, you never forget how it made you feel. **In networking, the feeling is the takeaway.** No matter what your DISC profile is, you can make someone feel good in your own, intentional way.

My objective was to stay on people's radar rather than falling off and losing out on the value of connections. I figured the best way to make this happen was to create a story that applied to every person: rich or poor, any gender, any ethnicity, extroverted or intro-verted, people-oriented or task-oriented, etc. In the period of 129 days when I met with over 1,000 people, I not only helped people grow their networks and revenue with my own connections, but as a byproduct, many friendships were created, experiences were had, and there was so much growth. Those one thousand meetings were worth more than I could have ever imagined. The lesson here is whether you can manage one thousand meetings or only ten, always be super intentional at each meeting – that's how you set yourself up to win.

Using DISC and Motivators to help you understand yourself and those you meet with can go a long way to making genuine connections. If you lead from your heart with the right motive and intent and consider people's needs before profit, you will naturally sell your product or service. **People don't buy products – they buy *you*.**

For DISC and Motivator assessment resources and coaching to help you learn to use this valuable tool to improve your networking, please go to https://zeroto100.io/disc.

Prioritize the Value You Give & The Goals You Make

I have five goals in life: The first was to become one of the most influential people in my city before age forty. That goal became a reality in May 2015 when I became one of the "Who's Who in Business in St. Charles, Missouri." I already had some credibility, but that increased my influence dramatically and my name grew even more in the community. The second goal was to become one of the most influential people in St. Louis. I achieved that in April 2016 when I was recognized as a "Top 100 St. Louisans to Succeed in Business." My third goal is to become one of the most influential people in North America. I am on track to make this happen with Zero to 100™. My fourth goal is to leave a global footprint. If I treat people right, this will happen. My fifth goal is to become a multimillionaire by age forty. After several failed network marketing ventures, I thought I had struck out with these goals. However, once I found the networking world, I knew this was the time to go for it. I met with people with the sincerest intent of building REAL-ation-ships while getting to know them personally and professionally.

I believe we only have one chance to make an impact and achieve our goals.

With that in mind, early in my career, I asked myself this question: What can I do for a living that will impact people glob-ally, possibly outlive me, and eternally add value to people's lives? And, boom! The answer became simple: **I want to teach business owners and sales professionals of all personalities across all**

**industries how to network effectively, which will grow their
relationships professionally and personally while enriching
their lives in the process.**

Ask yourself the same questions: what are your top five (or two
or three) goals in life? And how can you positively impact others?
If you prioritize your goals, work toward each one individually, and
help people in the process, the value you give can be organic and
measurable – even if it's as simple as sending a referral to a contact
that changes that person's life. With Zero to 100™, you are already
on the road to changing the world, one connection at a time.

The 51/49 Rule

The truth is that most networkers don't get enough referrals or
introductions to justify what they spend on networking. The average
networker spends $2,500 to $7,000 a year, which includes the
initial costs of joining a networking group, quarterly dues, weekly
dues, food and beverage, and gas and travel expenses. Most people
aren't seeing a good return on investment (ROI) with networking
and they end up approaching it with a scarcity mindset. But when
you prioritize the value you can *give* rather than the value you
can get from networking, you set yourself up for a much higher
networking return.

One principle I live by is called the 51/49 Rule – I always supply
51% of the value. **It's rare for someone to come to the table
with the intent to give rather than the intent to sell.** I want my
actions to always reflect the 51/49 Rule by referring more business
than I receive and connecting more people than ever before. Many
people *say* they want to help others in business through networking,
but very few actually do it. I know that if I continue getting to know
others and connecting people, my business will take care of itself,

which makes referring people the priority, whether or not someone comes through with a referral for me.

- When it comes to entrepreneurship, the truth is that most people drop the ball and don't follow through. We all live busy lives — it can be difficult when juggling so many tasks to remember to make a promised referral or an introduction. But when you don't treat these tasks as a priority, it devalues the time you put into networking (and the people you make promises to). So I decided to make a commitment to myself that I would never drop the ball when it came to helping others build their business. More networking groups are being started worldwide than there are people who teach, guide, and show you how to network. So I see this as my opportunity to shine and share a proven networking process that will help others.

Find Ways to Help Others

Networking is an environment of mingling entrepreneurs, business owners, and sales professionals looking to get to know one another and grow their networks, increase their revenue, and most importantly, create strong relationships. This might sound simple to accomplish, but it took me years to master the process of networking. With my systematic approach and curious nature, I began putting together a process that worked best for me. When I was just starting out and hadn't had much success, I sought to become a person of value others would like to sit down with — I wanted to be especially valuable to individuals who needed help getting their name out there.

Networking then became not only about meeting and connecting with people but also about finding ways to help others. **Effective networking is when you have the other person's best interest in mind 100% of the time.** When you learn about someone *professionally and personally,* you can develop a REAL-ationship based on more than business. It also makes your job to connect a person with others easier and it usually motivates that person to reciprocate. The more you get to know each person you meet with, the deeper your connections will be. For example, when you learn someone is married with children or single with a dog, you then have a reference for your own common interests, as well as when you mirror-match them with someone else in a similar place in life. Mirror-matching is essentially matching people based on personalities, values, and beliefs, rather than just professions or industries.

Once you understand someone on a deeper level, you should be able to look at your database or network and make introductions, connections, and referrals. But never introduce or refer just to connect or appear active. Making connections simply for the sake of it devalues your ability to make solid connections. Instead, do it to connect a person with a business owner who will potentially enhance and grow their business. When you take the time to get to know someone, you learn their needs and how you can help. If someone is new to networking, help this person learn the ropes and grow their own network with introductions to others who are great at connecting people. If you find a connection is looking for new clients and more revenue, then refer those who can use their products or services.

Depending on where you are in your life when you meet someone (Are you open and ready to give? Unsure but motivated? Preoccupied and closed-off?) determines that person's effectiveness in your network. It also changes how you positively or negatively affect the other person's life and business. Successful networking always comes from openness and genuine reciprocity that leads to helping others in business, which, in turn, leads to success in your business.

You will find when you give freely without the intent or expectation of receiving, amazing opportunities flow your way. It may take a while for the giving to come back around to you, but when good intentions are at the forefront of your interactions and connections with others, you *will* eventually reap what you sow. You will quickly feel more supported and encouraged when you have intentionality in your REAL-ationships.

When you take a meeting, your intention should be to fulfill the person's industry wheelhouse. A "wheelhouse" is a list of people in industries that make up their preferred network. For example, if a Realtor is looking to fill her wheelhouse with mortgage brokers, home inspectors, and hair stylists, try to connect her with those you know who are either in her wheelhouse or know someone who has those connections. To find out who your connection is looking for, simply ask which industry professionals will help fill that person's wheelhouse and focus your efforts on providing those that match. And be careful not to assume you know – you'd be surprised how successful non-conventional connections can be.

Another great way to assist in building someone's network is to help build diversity. This is one of the strongest ways to build *your* business too – by creating an open and diverse group of connections, you will expand your growth beyond your wildest dreams. Having a diverse network opens you up to opportunities and revenue you'd never have if you only did business with people who look, talk, and act like you. Through networking, you can make connections outside of your community, culture, ethnicity, gender, city, state, and country. Networking brings people together and creates cultural hubs; I've even seen it change people's prejudices (more on that later).

Bringing it Back to Coffee

Understanding and utilizing the Caffeinated Moment, DISC, and the Six Motivators, and what you bring to the table in networking will give you the best harvest of coffee cherries and yield the best fruit of your efforts in connecting with others.

CHAPTER 3

Sorting & Pulping the Cherry

Identifying Types of Networkers and Networking Groups

To get the best coffee beans, you need to sort the ripe cherries from the unripe then get rid of the pulp surrounding the ripe beans. In networking, you also need to sort the ripe cherries from the unripe so you can yield the best coffee beans – or in this case, great connections.

In this Chapter, the types of networking events are explained to help you better decide which approach suits your brand and personality and aligns with your business goals. You will be introduced to the F.O.R.M. Technique, which provides you with questions that flow nicely to get in and out of conversations while still learning about each other. You will also be able to identify what kind of networker you might be based on DISC, as well as the different types of networking events you may align with based on your internal Motivators.

The F.O.R.M. Technique

For most people, conversations with strangers can be awkward and uncomfortable. Before you go out on the open floor of networking and socialize, you should know the F.O.R.M. Technique to gain the most out of each interaction and maximize your time. This is a group of topics that resonate universally with anyone and comfortably guide you in and out of conversations. I had been asking this series of questions for years before I learned there was an acronym to help conversations be less awkward and more productive in building REAL-ationships...

> **F — Friends and family** – Ask about friends and family (people love to talk about themselves and the people closest to them).
>
> **O — Occupation** – Ask what they do for a living and about their company/business.
>
> **R — Recreation** – Ask what your connection likes to do in their spare time (walk the dog, watch movies, go to baseball games, travel ...).
>
> **M — Message** – Share a snippet about your company (explained in Chapter 3, Step 4 in the Elevator Blueprint).

As you practice the F.O.R.M. Technique more and more in a live setting, you will add more of your personality and it won't sound so robotic. Practice makes perfect and every detail should be rehearsed so the conversation flows smoothly. Financial advisors study prior to taking the Series 7 and Series 66 exams, doctors study for their board exams, videographers spend hours becoming skilled with video editing, and school teachers rehearse how they welcome their class and parents on the first day of school. Therefore, to be an excellent networker, you need to practice asking the right questions to get to know the right people. When you approach networking with purpose and the right intent (meaning zero ulterior motive with no bait and switch) and treat it as part of your business, it will reward you as such. Building REAL-ationships all starts with asking the right questions. And, once you master asking the right questions, you need to follow through.

For example, Susan, who is in your network, is going to be a great referral for "Joe Builder." She would catapult his business!

You're excited to send Susan to Joe as a referral as soon as you have time. But first, when you meet with Joe, you have to tell him all about what you do and who you're looking for. You run out of time to mention Sue, but you'll get to it later. At your next meeting after Joe, "Betty's Boutique" has one person in her network to introduce you to but you talk on and on and don't get to learn about her referral for you. At the end of the day, due to poor listening skills and being preoccupied with thoughts of what you wanted to share about yourself, you ran out of time and missed the chance to send the referral to Joe and make Betty's connection. You missed the opportunity to use the F.O.R.M. Technique with Betty to learn who she is and find that potential connection for one another. Joe missed out, Betty missed out, and you missed out. The lesson here is that it's imperative to learn how to:

- Maximize your time.
- Show proper respect by taking the time to learn about your connections.
- Take an interest in and follow up with the introductions/referrals they send
- Follow through and send the referrals they need from your network.
- Focus on how you can help them.

The F.O.R.M. technique will keep you on track and ensure you get the right information about each person.

"If you collect 20 business cards in a day with the hope
of getting one sale, you're doing it wrong."

– Carol Luckett

Networking is not about how many people you meet and how many clients you get – it's about helping the people around

you and helping your community grow. When you approach each event or meeting with the mindset of how many people you can help through the people you know (even if you're new to networking, you know people) you are networking for the right reasons.

The Five Types of Networkers

As you enter the world of networking, it's important to understand each type of networker you might encounter to know the signs of both a self-focused networker and a networker who puts others first. This will keep you from wandering off the path of becoming a great networker. Here are five basic types of networkers.

1. The Bottom-feeder Networker

This is a common, universal kind of networker. Bottom-feeders only see networking as a numbers game and not a relationship-building strategy that can create lasting referral partners. Things to watch for:

- They hand out and collect as many business cards/contact information as possible.
- They have little understanding of the power of reciprocity.
- They have their own best interests at heart; don't consider the needs of others.
- They want quantity over quality; always trying to sell, sell, sell.
- Don't expect many, if any, referrals from this networker.
- You'll leave a meeting with a bottom-feeder networker feeling that this person only came with their best interests in mind.
- In coffee terms, this networker is a bitter, harsh cup that's tough to swallow.

THE BOTTOM-FEEDER NETWORKER
Bitter & Harsh

I've had many experiences with bottom-feeder networkers, but one example stands out from the rest. At a St. Louis area Chamber of Commerce luncheon, I spoke with a person at my table who is involved with eight other Chambers and two other networking organizations – and this individual never misses a single meeting. When we met for a Caffeinated Moment, I provided several introductions and referrals, and since then, there have been few introductions and referrals I've received in return. This person is a member of multiple organizations yet hasn't taken the time to form REAL-ationships with anyone and doesn't believe in having multiple meetings with people. This bottom-feeder networker is out for selfish gain and not interested in helping others grow their businesses. In Chapter 8, you'll learn how to manage these meetings and not think of them as a waste of time – everyone you spend time with has an impact on your life, so don't let bottom feeders discourage your networking attempts.

2. The Serial Networker

These networkers are in a ton of groups. You will see their faces at all the ribbon-cutting ceremonies and in all the photos because they attend every event and are in it for the "social game" or status. You'll find:

- Retirees who are in it to make friends and for social interaction.

- Those who "double date" as a networking activity (no kidding!).
- The occasional introduction or referral, but most have the sole intent of being social.
- They're more focused on the next bright and shiny thing rather than the long game of building relationships.
- You'll leave a meeting (if you even get one) with a serial networker feeling curious about how committed they are to their current businesses and if this person will still be doing the same thing in the next six months or be onto the next new exciting venture.
- In coffee terms, this networker is a rather bland and neutral cup of coffee.

THE SERIAL NETWORKER
Bland & Neutral

Not too long ago, I met a serial networker who attends networking organization events but doesn't usually join. When we had our Caffeinated Moment, it was an incredible meeting. This individual "believes in reciprocity," but over the course of a year, I only received about four introductions. This connection networks on both sides of the Mississippi River – in Missouri and Illinois – so the potential is there, but the introductions I receive are neither consistent, good, nor reliable. This person is warm and welcoming but not that productive of a networker and therefore falls into the serial networker category. Again, there is still value in meeting this person, you just need to manage the meeting and follow-up as it makes sense. You'll find more details on this in Chapter 8.

3. The Newbie Networker

New networkers are trying to figure out how to build better bridges of collaboration that create flourishing reciprocity and sustain their network. They have just started networking or have been networking for several months, had time to reflect on their networking experiences, and are beginning to understand the different types of groups. These networkers:

- May be seasoned in business but brand new to networking.
- Are learning how to focus on the quality of connections rather than quantity of connections alone.
- Search for ways to maximize their efforts by evaluating the networking groups they're part of, focusing on the ones with the best ROI.
- Are firecrackers – they may be new, but they're ready to up their game to be the best networker they can be.
- Don't fully understand the networking world yet but they're quickly becoming awesome networkers.
- Give consistent introductions and referrals.
- In coffee terms, this networker is a bold and flavorful cup that excites the palette.

THE NEWBIE NETWORKER
Bold & Acidic

I recently met a newbie networker through a St. Louis networking organization. This person is introverted, doesn't know about all the networking groups or networking basics yet, but also wants to be the best networker possible. Since we met, this connection has consistently given me introductions and referrals. This type of networker is a great teaching opportunity; a way to shine and reap REAL-ationship rewards, it may just take patience.

> **Tip:** Introverted? New to Networking? To network more efficiently in person, take a wingperson with you! Go to events with a friend, co-worker, or referral partner and ask that person to introduce you to others. It helps ease the tension and you'll find yourself opening up more and more. You might even set up a Caffeinated Moment before the day is done. And if you're networking virtually, which is predominantly one-on-one meetings, look at it as an opportunity to have more control over who you connect with and when.

One book that I strongly recommend is *The Introvert's Edge to Networking* by Matthew Pollard with Derek Lewis.[6] Written by a networking acquaintance of mine, this book is a game-changer for introverts when paired with everything you are going to learn in my book.

4. The Hobbyist Networker

These networkers occasionally attend networking events for great conversations and a good time meeting people. They have a hard time staying focused on one business and tend to be involved in several different business ventures. Hobbyists:

- Typically have their own best interests at heart.
- Always look for the latest and greatest; the next best thing.
- Will rarely, if ever, refer or make an introduction, but if they do, it'll be rock solid.
- When you sit down with a hobbyist, you'll be pitched everything in their arsenal, which might confuse you and make it difficult to refer business.
- In coffee terms, a hobbyist is a cup of strong coffee that's unpredictable.

THE HOBBYIST NETWORKER
Mellow & Sweet

I had a hobbyist networker add me on Facebook, and when someone adds me on Facebook, I typically send out a message of gratitude for the request. This networker didn't respond to my message. Shortly after, we met at a networking event and this person invited me to a meeting over coffee. During our Caffeinated Moment, I learned that they have a traditional 9-to-5 job and only attend networking events during off-hours. Because of this, I don't get introductions or referrals from him/her often, but I did receive one rock-solid introduction that turned out to be gold! The hobbyist networker is good to follow up with a few times a year and casually stay in touch with. You never know when your referrals might be just what this person needs and the occasional referral from him/her can turn out to be gold.

5. The Connector

Connectors are living the power of networking – everybody strives to be a connector! They are constantly thinking about the introductions they're going to make and who can help who. These powerful, caring people:

- Go into events with the intent of bringing value to everyone they meet.
- Create a brand byproduct that benefits their revenue and network.
- Tend to be submissive, loyal, principle-oriented, selfless, and always have a person's best interest in mind without the "what's in it for me" mentality.
- Give consistent and reliable introductions and referrals.
- In coffee terms, connectors are a cup of balanced full-bodied yet mellow coffee.

THE CONNECTOR NETWORKER
Full-bodied & Balanced

One of my connections, who has been deep into networking for at least seven years, is one of the best examples of a connector networker. When I first met with this person, I received nearly ten-strong connections. This person runs a networking group with 50-60 big networking players at each event and is a connecting machine who always considers how to help others. This connector networker is an obvious choice for regular meetings – just be sure you're reciprocating and offering quality meetings.

Note that these types of networkers are harder to identify in virtual group networking meetings because behaviors that are naturally observable in a face-to-face group setting are all but lost in this context. To get a better idea for the type of networker a person would be in an in-person group setting, I recommend having a one-on-one Caffeinated Moment with this person and asking the following questions:

- Are you new to networking?
- How long have you been networking?
- What do you like and dislike about networking?
- What would you like to be better at in networking?

By asking these questions, you will either receive a selfish answer or a selfless answer. A selfish answer means they could be a bottom-feeder or serial networker. If it's a selfless answer, it could be a newbie networker or connector. A hobbyist networker can go either way. However, you still won't get the full picture until you can meet with that person face-to-face.

Everyone you meet is your future because you can truly learn something from everybody. You always have the potential to meet someone who may lead you to the one person that takes your business to the next level.

What Kind of Networker Are You?

Ideally, we all want to be connectors in networking, but the learning curve can be a little longer for some personalities. When it comes to connectors, the people who generally have the easiest time fulfilling this role are more extroverted, people-oriented personalities. Let's take another look at DISC concerning networking types, and remember – we are all a blend of the four behaviors and these behaviors can be harder to observe in virtual settings

High "D"

High "D" types are dominant, direct, results-oriented, extroverted networkers who may have a difficult time because they are task-oriented and therefore may treat networking more like a task or a means-to-an-end. They may seem impatient and don't like to wait around to get results – and networking is a long game. You see many "Ds" as bottom-feeder networkers or hobbyists as it is all about the task of getting business; they may seem egotistical and not open to the ongoing learning process of networking. However, don't be scared off by the results-driven nature. If you have common goals, you can establish a great rapport. "Ds" can prove to be great referral partners. If you feel you may be a High "D" networker, here are some tips:

- Be patient.
- Make sure you follow up with people.
- Get a list of people who are going to be at an event beforehand if possible.
- Don't give up on networking because you're not getting results right away.
- Realize that others may be more relationship-focused.

For High "D" networkers, the Zero to 100™ Platform is great for getting efficient introductions and referrals, as well as being able to track results.

High "I"

If you're a High "I" type – influential, interpersonal, popular, and trusting – being a connector comes naturally to you. "I" types love networking! But for those who are extra chatty, they may be more interested in networking just for fun, think "serial networkers."

Tips for High "I" networkers:
- Don't get caught up talking to one person for too long.
- Set goals for networking and stay focused on those goals – particularly in a virtual setting.
- Have a good follow-up system in place after so you don't get distracted and forget.
- Recognize that others may be more results-focused or move at a slower pace.

For High "I" networkers, the Zero to 100™ Platform is great to connect you to a lot of people looking for REAL-ationships and to hold you accountable for following up and staying on track with your networking goals.

High "S"

High "S" types – steady, stable, and routine-driven – also tend to be more introverted and, therefore, may have a harder time because they're not as comfortable guiding a conversation. However, "S" networkers are skilled at developing lasting relationships because of their consistent follow-through. "S" types fall into the serial networker or newbie networker categories. They can be fantastic networkers but may take longer to warm to the process or a room full of people.

Tips for High "S" networkers:
- Find a familiar group of people to get to know over time.
- Join a structured group.
- Learn a couple of good questions to guide conversations.
- Don't be afraid to ask someone for their business card/contact information.
- Recognize others may want to move at a faster pace and work the room – or in a virtual setting – talk more than you.
- Stay flexible and allow for some free time when scheduling meetings virtually.

For High "S" networkers, the Zero to 100™ Platform will help you network with more structure and find a good group of people to network with.

High "C"

High "C" types tend to be both introverted and task-oriented, as well as conscientious and correct, therefore they may have the hardest time in networking. They're primarily concerned with the goal of networking but may not like being around people at all. Many "Cs" may be bottom-feeder networkers or hobbyists – in any case, they're concerned with how they can systematize their networking.

Tips for High "C" networkers:
- Gather as much data as possible about a networking group to be sure the people you want to talk to are in that group.
- Educate yourself on how to network effectively in a virtual setting.
- Prepare a few good questions to guide conversations.
- Recognize others are more people-focused, may move at a faster pace, and are less concerned with accuracy.

For the High "C" networker, the Zero to 100™ Platform is fantastic for tracking data and measuring the return on investment (ROI).

Based on your DISC profile, there are different recommendations to more effectively work and network from home. If you're interested in learning more about how to communicate better and network in a virtual setting based on your DISC style, you can take this free assessment from TTI by following the prompts on our site: https://zeroto100.io/

Remember that networking to become a connector is a marathon, not a sprint. And keep in mind, in the same way that people train to run a marathon, networkers must practice diligently to become a true, natural connector. Becoming a connector is all about the *quality* of your character and learning to recognize and adapt your behavior to others' behaviors to create comfortable connections. To learn more about the role of character in business, I recommend reading my friend Larry Cowsert's book, *Character: Lessons Learned from a Character About Having Character.* This is a collection of interviews from people with extraordinary character, and the stories prove that humility and respect for others are essential to building a legacy, a reputation, and a strong network of REAL-ationships.

Good character is imperative to developing REAL-ationships and sets you up for premium growth in networking.

April 11, 2018, with Larry Cowsert and his book
Character: Lessons Learned from a Character About Having Character[7]
at the St. Louis Bread Company in Westport, St. Louis.

Structured vs. Unstructured Networking

There is a wide variety of networking groups available to business owners and sales professionals, and each appeals to a certain personality and behavioral type with certain goals. While each networking group is different, they all gather with similar intent and fall somewhere on the spectrum between structured and unstructured.

Structured Networking

Structured networking is perfect for people who like order, outlines, and agendas as it offers more guidance and direction. There is typically a monthly and/or annual fee and an occasional event fee.

- Events generally begin with open-floor networking where people socialize before the main event or meeting agenda, followed by an agenda where everyone is seated and may eat a meal while listening to a speaker.
- Sometimes events are timed to keep to a rigid schedule.
- Business attire is typically expected and there may be expectations (or even requirements) to refer or make introductions within the group, depending on its exclusivity.
- Structured networking groups work well for business owners/salespeople who rely on referrals for most of their business, appreciate routine and predictability, and value the exclusivity of a group that limits the number of members per industry, location, or interest.

Examples of structured networking groups: BNI (Business Network International)[8], Chambers of Commerce, Christian Business Leaders, Master Networks, and so on. For a longer list of networking groups, see section vi. in the Appendix.

Unstructured Networking

This type of networking event is popular for people on a tight schedule because you may come and go as you please and meet as many or few people as you like in a relaxed environment. These events may or may not have a fee associated with them.

- Events are more relaxed and come in many different variations.
- Attire is generally casual and there is no schedule or agenda to uphold.
- The unstructured atmosphere provides newbies a chance to watch and determine who they'd like to approach. It also

allows them to participate in a group conversation where a simple nod or laugh goes a long way — especially if they don't know what to say.

• The most unstructured formats typically come in the form of morning coffee or happy hours, which take place before work or in the early evening and might appeal to those who are building a business around their 9-to-5 job.

The Caffeinated Moment version of an unstructured event would be meeting someone to play golf or tennis. In this intimate networking setting, you can learn about one another on a more personal level. If that relationship is developed properly, you will successfully come out with two things: a new friend and a new skill or hobby.

Examples of unstructured networking groups: morning coffee, happy hours, charity golf outings or events, volunteer scenarios, recreational sports, civic groups, and large local celebrations.

The only way to tell the difference between a structured and unstructured networking group in a virtual setting is whether there's an agenda or not.

Within the structured and unstructured networking events, there are a few more specifics like the Association, Activity, Closed, and Open groups, and those with inclusivity and exclusivity. Once you understand the types of networking groups, then you have what you need to find the one(s) that best suits you. Most of these groups allow visitors, so feel free to explore until you find the one that fits your personality and goals.

1. Association Networking Groups

This falls on the structured side of the networking spectrum. Association networking gains business through the social aspect of a specific group setting. You'll find these groups tied to common interests such as:

- Self-Development – Landmark, Toastmasters, Mastermind, yoga
- Professional – Chambers of Commerce, engineers, writers, lawyers, software developers
- Religion – Church groups, temple groups, mosque groups, humanist groups
- Competitive sports/games – racquetball, basketball, hockey, bowling, softball, chess, etc.

Many people find this form of networking easier and more comfortable as the group members hold similar interests – making for smoother conversation. From my experiences with association networking groups, people get comfortable with the structure and familiarity of these groups, so it becomes natural for them to make referrals with people in the group. However, for an association networking group to grow – or any networking group, for that matter – it's important to refer to the person, not to the organization. Connecting people based on personality, rather than referring only to be loyal to a group, will strengthen the network rather than simply sustain it.

2. Activity Networking Groups

Activity networking is networking while enjoying a popular hobby. This is one of the most unstructured networking types out there. You've heard the adage that more business is done on a golf course than in the boardroom – that's activity networking. When you invite a potential client or partner to a more social event such as a sporting event or golf outing, you create a more relaxed environment in which to conduct business and build a personal relationship.

Examples of activity networking:
- Attending a sporting event.
- Participating in recreational sports – golf, running, biking, yoga, etc.

- Enjoying cultural arts – theatre, opera, galleries, music venues.
- Socializing – going to the theater, the gym, out to dinner, etc.

When I had a networking meeting at Topgolf®, a large golf complex with a variety of games, I realized I couldn't take notes during this meeting because my hands would be busy with a golf club. As a new networker, this might have turned me off because I'm the kind of person who finds it important to take notes during my meetings (High Theoretical). However, what I like about activity networking is that it helps people relax and talk more personally about themselves rather than their business. This type of social environment is really helpful for building REAL-ationships.

3. Closed Networking Groups/Exclusivity

Similar to association networking, closed networking is structured. It's also more exclusive – the groups limit the number of individuals within similar industries. Keeping a tight group with a limited number of industry-specific leaders can help you succeed by receiving introductions and referrals within the group. This group is designed to create referral partners to help grow your business. However, referrals in closed networking often stay within the group, which means if you're in a specialized industry or have a unique skill set, you may feel limited by networking only within the group. It's okay to grow your network outside of the group; there's plenty of business to go around.

Examples of closed networking (there are hundreds of these groups):

- Business Network International (BNI)
- Master Networks
- TEAM Referral Networks

While closed networking groups are designed to help you succeed with exclusivity and are often a perfect fit for your goals, make sure the one you choose expands rather than limits the growth of your network. Connect with the people in the group based on REAL-ationships first; this strengthens everyone's network.

4. Open Networking Group

Open networking is unstructured, more relaxed, and non-exclusive or inclusive. In open networking, there is an abundance-mindset culture that makes people excited to share and meet. It's generally a bubbly atmosphere where you find an excited, forward-thinking group that welcomes all.

Examples of open networking:
- Happy hours
- Breakfast/coffee networking
- Meetup groups

In my opinion, like activity networking, open networking encourages people to speak more casually to one another, expediting the REAL-ationship building process. It's awesome to have multiple people in the same industries in the room because they each bring different personalities. In open networking, the abundance mindset enables people to refer to personalities first rather than an organization.

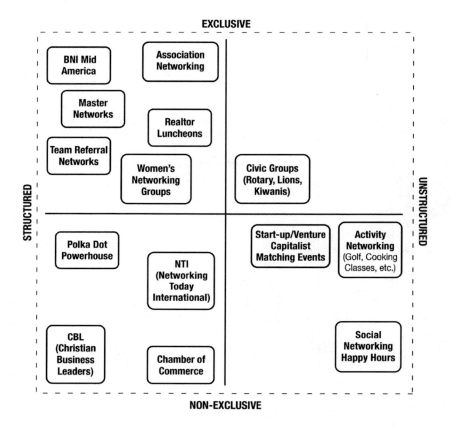

What Type of Networking Group Suits You?

You will find people of every DISC style in networking groups and those with certain Motivators may be drawn to specific types of groups. With your new DISC and Motivator knowledge, you might be trying to figure out which of these networking groups will be the best fit for you. This breakdown of which groups are likely suitable to each Motivator may help.

Theoretical – High theoretical motivator types seek networking groups where there's an opportunity to learn. Intellectually motivated people are drawn to Association Networking Groups like Mastermind, Rotary, Landmark, and Toastmasters because they provide a presentation every meeting.

Utilitarian – Resourceful people have a high utilitarian motivator and look for groups that offer an ROI for their business. Business Network International (BNI) is a prime example of a group that attracts utilitarian folks because there is a measurable system of passing referrals. Resourceful people will watch their ROI closely. Association and Closed Networking groups are typically best for these people.

Aesthetic – People with high aesthetic motivators want networking groups centered around the quality of experience. Activity and Open Networking groups are created to share an experience and draw the aesthetic crowd. For example, wine tasting clubs, hiking groups, or other types of activity networking.

Social – Altruistic people have strong social motivators and seek networking groups that serve people and causes. Therefore, Association or Activity Networking groups with a greater good mission such as the Rotary Club, Kiwanis, or the Lion's Club are best for socially motivated people.

Individualistic – Closed Networking is most suitable for highly individualistic people due to its exclusivity. People with high individualistic motivators will be drawn to exclusive, membership-based networking groups such as BNI or Master Networks. However, they can also be non-joiners if they don't see their identity within the group.

Traditional – People with high traditional motivators will be drawn to more traditional, value-based networking groups. Unlike people with individualistic motivators, the traditionally motivated *are* joiners. Closed and Association Networking groups are typically best for this group. Examples include Chambers of Commerce (focused on the businesses in a specific community) and Veteran's networking groups.

Find the Right Networking Group for You*

*A Note About Group Networking During And in the Wake of the 2020 Pandemic

If you are just starting to network during or soon after the 2020 pandemic, joining a group is one of the most effective uses of your time. However, you must know that when groups are not meeting in person or have very limited capacity, you cannot get the full picture of the networking group dynamics. COVID completely changed how we approach networking. It has not only forced us to connect through screens but has also changed why we're networking.

The pandemic turned networking into a necessity. Forced virtual networking does not enable you to network from a natural and stable state, as you have no other choice but to network through a screen that is limiting and even emotional. That's why, when virtual networking is the only option, I recommend focusing on individual networking while keeping your commitment to your networking group until meeting in person is possible again. Members are the cornerstone of the group – they drive brand awareness, referrals, introductions, and revenue. When people are forced to be away from meeting in groups for a long time, they will gravitate towards groups when it's safe to meet in person. But as long as it's not safe to meet in person, focus on truly connecting to individual people and getting to know them. You will learn more about the art of connecting with people individually in Chapter 6.

When we're able to connect in groups in person again, selecting the right networking group will be the single most important task in the life of a new networker. If you are just starting out or have hit a plateau and are looking to light a fire under your existing business, take time to choose the right group. It can make a *huge difference* in your immediate success. Here's how.

Define your goals, personality and values, your mission and/or vision, and your brand or business, then identify a group of people in a setting that meets your needs and fits your principles, values, and synergy. Also, choose one where your personality benefits the group as well.

If you are a light-hearted, happy-go-lucky business owner who enjoys being around people, you might want to look into attending an unstructured event first. This type will best suit your need for fun and fellowship, especially if you are new to networking and aren't entirely certain of what to do just yet. You will be exposed to a diverse group of business owners in a relaxed environment where there are zero expectations other than casual conversation with as many or as few people as you choose. You are in control of your own time at this kind of event and may come and go at your discretion. For those with more reserved personalities or those new to networking, there will be groups of people networking where you can step in and casually join the conversation. This is an amazing opportunity to share your business (your 30-second or 45-second elevator speech) with multiple people at once without having to hold down a single conversation right away.

The group setting also allows others who are more seasoned and well-known networkers to introduce you to those passing by and keep you from the awkward individual conversation if you are not ready for that yet. I recommend making at least one attempt at your first networking event to pursue a one-on-one conversation and practice the F.O.R.M. Technique to work on your skills.

Don't worry about messing up – every networker has been the new person at an event before and we all know how uncomfortable it is at first! Just be yourself and share your personality and business with enthusiasm. You'll become much more confident and comfortable speaking to people one-on-one, if not this time, definitely next time. No networker can ever be an expert because every new person you meet can teach you something new about networking. To refine your networking skills, you have to be willing to constantly tweak and adapt your approach based on who's sitting across from you.

If you are more task-oriented and/or introverted, chances are that a more structured networking group would serve you well. Following a strict agenda and limiting interaction within a set group of people on a regular basis could appeal to "D", "S", and "C" types for different reasons. For "Ds," structured networking may satisfy their need for a fast-paced, task-oriented environment. For "S" types, structured networking could be more comfortable since there are set schedules and an opportunity to build relationships at their own pace. And structured networking meshes well with "Cs" for the same reasons as both "D" and "S" types. Some "I" behavior styles may even appreciate structured networking for the chance to build rapport within a group. If you're not sure which networking group to start with, start by visiting groups that you believe are aligned with your behaviors and values.

In these networking groups and events, you will encounter competition. Competition is nothing to fear or shy away from. Introduce yourself to your competitor and be interested in what they do. Often, competition can become a plentiful referral source or partnership, hence the saying, "there's no such thing as competition." You're not going to attract everyone and each business is only going to attract a certain group of the population. What may not be an ideal customer for you may be perfect for your competitor. You then show integrity and value to the person asking to do business with you by referring him or her to the other company. That's why two people in the same industry who serve the same demographic can both benefit from Zero to 100™ networking. Different personalities make different introductions and referrals and can fulfill many business needs together.

Knowing When to Stay in a Networking Group and When to Go

It can be difficult finding the best place for you in networking. Sometimes it's just a matter of sticking it out in a new group and giving yourself some time to warm up to the people, but sometimes that new group may just not be the right fit for you. Here are some signs of whether you should stay or go:

How to Know When to Stay	How to Know When to Go
• You're getting along with most people and your presence is celebrated. • The group is very inclusive. • It's a welcoming environment for everyone, especially for guests. • The number of warm introductions and referrals you're receiving outweighs the time, effort, and/or financial commitment you're investing in the group. • Most everyone in the group seems to be receiving warm introductions and referrals, not just a select few. • Every member's opinion is welcome. • You feel you're truly gaining something from the group that you would not otherwise get if you were not a member.	• You see cliques within the group. • You witness the person running the meeting bashing or belittling other networking groups. • Members of the group seem disconnected or don't get along with one another. • As you meet with folks, you find out they aren't having meetings with members of the group to build relationships (it indicates the group is more transactional than relational). • The number of warm introductions or referrals exchanged within the group seems low – unless it's a socially oriented group and the focus is not as ROI-driven. • The group puts more focus on members than the guests who attend.

Here is a list of several national and international networking groups and two podcasts that may help you find your ideal networking group. (I do not endorse these for any reason other than they exist to help people connect!). There are also many local groups; be sure to locate those in your area and visit them as well.

BNI – Business Networking International
https://www.bni.com/

WNA – Women's Network Australia
https://www.womensnetwork.com.au/

Rockstar Connect
https://rockstarconnect.com/

Center Sphere – The Network;
www.CenterSphere.com

Master Networks
https://www.masternetworks.com/new-home-page

NTI – Networking Today International
https://networkingtodayintl.com/

Diverse Force
https://www.diverseforce.com/

Team Referral Networks
https://teamreferralnetwork.com/

PDP – Polka Dot Powerhouse
https://www.polkadotpowerhouse.com/

WEW – Women Empowering Women
http://www.wewnational.com

IWant2Network (Central London, England)
www.IWant2Network.com

Travis Chappell – Build Your Network
https://travischappell.com/podcast/

Robbie Samuels – On The Schmooze
www.OnTheSchmooze.com

Bringing it Back to Coffee

The ability to identify different types of networkers and the different groups where they gather provides an understanding of how to connect better with the right people – it helps you identify and sort the ripe coffee bean cherries in networking for the smoothest cup of coffee.

Study Results: Networking Events & Improvements

Participants in the study attended a broad range of networking event types:

- 67% participated in relationship-maintenance events
- 62% participated in Chamber of Commerce and BNI types of events
- 46% participated in Entrepreneurial types of events
- 44% participated in Workshop/Seminar events
- 38% participated in Happy Hour events
- 36% participated in Conferences
- 21% participated in Corporate events

The types of networking events participants regularly attended did not have an effect on how strongly their networking and business benefited from Zero to 100™. Again, the improvements were always based on how closely they followed the principles within the book.

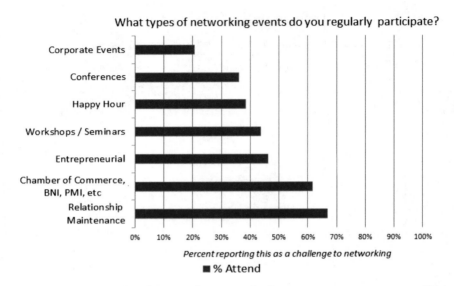

What types of networking events do you regularly participate?

Percent reporting this as a challenge to networking
■ % Attend

Participants in the study attended, on average, two or three networking events per week. This was generally consistent throughout the study.

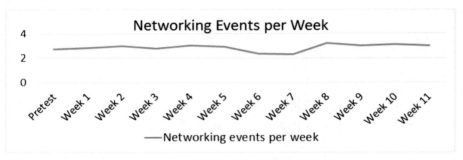

Networking Events per Week

——Networking events per week

Too often, people stop putting effort into networking because they find challenges, such as the time investment of finding reciprocal relationships, to be overwhelming. Participants of the study identified that the book helped them improve their ability to deal with these challenges quite dramatically.

Participants found that the time investment was 311% easier, and finding reciprocal relationships was 384% easier by the end of the study.

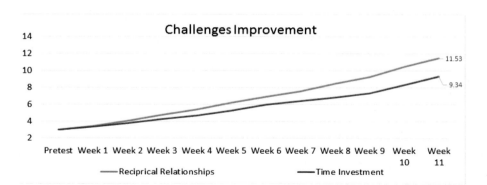

CHAPTER 4

Fermenting & Drying the Coffee Beans

The Elevator Speech

The next step in the coffee-making process is fermenting and drying the beans. This is what gives the coffee its depth and flavor. In networking, this step is called the **Elevator Speech**. In this Chapter, I'll explain what an elevator speech is and give you the proper elements of a good elevator speech, a blueprint to craft your own, and the different types of speeches you'll hear while networking.

What is an Elevator Speech?

An elevator speech is your prepared 30-, 45-, or 60-second commercial in which you share a snapshot of:

- Your work and/or company
- Why you are unique/your attention grabber
- How you solve problems your competition can't
- Who you help/your target market
- How you deliver products and services to that market
- Who you are searching for to grow your business

A succinct, well-developed elevator speech is imperative to efficiently work the room and best present yourself and your business in meetings, events, and in smaller networking groups. When networking, once you've opened the door to conversation with your elevator speech, **be specific about the kinds of introductions you are looking for so others can best refer you.**

When you first meet someone and see the chance to deliver your well-oiled elevator speech, this is your only opportunity to make a first impression and attract someone who *wants* to sit down with you to learn more about you and what you do. It's called an "elevator speech," after all, because it should be short and concise enough for you to deliver it in an elevator ride with someone. When your elevator speech is effective, you show everyone in the room that you respect their time because you finish in the time allotted – 30, 45, or 60 seconds. Clear and concise communication of your purpose and needs is necessary to attract more business.

The 30-, 45-, and 60-Second Elevator Speech Blueprint

1. Greet everyone according to the time of day (Good morning, afternoon, evening).

   It sets the tone by showing your strong presence in the room and your gratitude for being there.

2. State your name (I am _____ _____).

3. State your company (I am with ..., I do ..., or My company is ...).

   Note: Combine #2 and #3 for better flow.

   Ex. I am Joseph Luckett with Company ABC.

4. Share an attention grabber.

   Share a snippet of what makes your company special that will immediately captivate the room. Your attention grabber should be abridged if you're not delivering the full 60-second speech.

   Ex. 60 seconds: I am Joseph Luckett with Company ABC. Several partners and I have scaled a concept from zero to $2 billion in gross revenue in eight years. We did that by introducing the world's first acid-free organic coffee to the market.

Ex. 45 seconds: I am Joseph Luckett with Company ABC, the world's first acid-free organic coffee on the market.

Ex. 30 seconds: I am Joseph Luckett with Company ABC introducing organic, acid-free coffee.

5. If it helps clarify what you do, mention your competition briefly and how you differ and give three top-of-mind problems or pain points that you solve.

    Do this to add credibility. If your business is new to the area and you are just beginning to branch out into the market, it may help to do a quick competitive comparison. This also works if your company is a smaller firm but can handle everything an enterprise-sized group can. For example, if you're in-home health care and there's a well-known national company that does what you do, it can help to say, "My company, ABC Home Health Care, is similar to Well Care Health, only we are locally owned and offer many specialty services for extra care."

    If you're delivering a 60-second speech, and you have time, fit in three examples. For a 45-second speech, give two examples, and if it's a 30-second speech, just give one example. Here are my own examples, plus the home health care example.

    Ex. 60 seconds: Regular coffee can cause jitters, acid reflux, and the shakes.

    Ex. 60 seconds: Other home health care companies have higher caregiver turnover, lack the personal touch, and are less available when needed.

    Ex. 45 seconds: Regular coffee causes jitters and shakes.

    Ex. 45 seconds: Other home health care agencies tend to be less personal and less available.

Ex. 30 seconds: Regular coffee causes jitters.

Ex. 30 seconds: Other home health care agencies often lack the personal touch.

6. Express reasons why you/your company offer(s) unique value. This is your chance to set your business apart from the competition you've just described. If you are just as capable of handling the same tasks as your competitors, then share why you do it better, faster, or how you work with a more personalized relationship. This is your shot to sell your products or services. In a 60-second speech, list four or five facts that make your business different. In the 45-second speech, keep it to three points, and in your 30-second speech keep it to two points — and one of those points should be considerate of who's in the audience.

Ex. 60 seconds: Our coffee provides the following nutrition…
- *Three times more antioxidants than blueberries*
- *Eight times more omega-3 than salmon*
- *15 times more magnesium than broccoli*
- *Seven times more Vitamin C than an orange*
- *And six times more calcium than a glass of milk*

Ex. 45 seconds: Our coffee is soy, dairy, and gluten-free with a PH level of 7.35, which is equivalent to one bottle of Fiji water, and it has three times more protein than peanut butter.

Ex. 30 seconds: Our coffee has the same PH level as a bottle of Fiji water and _____.

I'd customize the above benefits based on what I think my audience's internal motivators are. For example, someone with a strong *theoretical motivation* will want to know the nutritional facts about the product, whereas someone with a strong *social motivation* will want to know that Company ABC has a non-profit that supports educating children.

7. Describe how you get your product or service into the marketplace.

   This is how you entice people to try your product or service. Depending on the length of your speech, you can go into more detail about how you market what you're selling. Do you do free sample marketing? Or offer a free assessment?

   Ex. 60 seconds: Remember back in the early '90s when AOL gave out the free CD sample? We do the same thing, but instead of a disk, it's free coffee samples. Who here knows Folgers? They made their name from free-sample marketing – by knocking on doors and brewing cups of coffee.

   Ex. 45 seconds: Give either AOL or Folgers example depending on the audience.

   Ex. 30 seconds: We do free sample marketing.

8. Describe your ideal customer/client/referral partner.

   Share your consumer base/target market so your audience understands who you seek to do business with and they begin thinking of who they can introduce to you. What kind of introductions are you looking for? Are you looking for residential or commercial? Business-to-consumer (B2C) or business-to-business (B2B) introductions?

   In the full 60-second speech, list up to four introductions you seek and three locations where you want to network. In 45 seconds, list only three introductions and two areas, and in 30 seconds, just mention one introduction and one area where you want to network.

Ex. 60 seconds: I'm looking for introductions to bankers, nutritionists, stay-at-home moms, and real estate agents in St. Louis, Los Angeles, and London.

Ex. 45 seconds: I'm looking for introductions to bankers, nutritionists, and stay-at-home moms in St. Louis and Los Angeles.

Ex. 30 seconds: I'm looking for introductions to nutritionists in the St. Louis area.

9. Share what or who you are looking for in a customer or referral partner.

   Be industry-specific (chiropractor, attorney, etc.), value-specific, culture-specific, or even person-specific. If you are looking for an introduction to a particular individual, now is the time to state that person's name. The more specifics you provide, especially around industry and network, the more likely you are to receive fantastic introductions. (This piece of networking is called "Tour Guiding" and will be covered in Chapter 6.) In your 60-second speech, give three industries, three individuals, and three different cities. In your 45-second and 30-second speeches, give only one of each.

10. As you get ready to close, thank everyone, especially the person who invited you for the opportunity to share.

    Ex: Thank you for having me and to Jim for inviting me to this wonderful group.

11. Then, state your name again.

    Remind them again who you are since you have just WOW'd them and sent their mind racing with who they can introduce you to.

    Ex: My name is Joseph ...

12. State the name of your company again.

Top-of-mind awareness is important to keep your name fresh on their minds and gives them another opportunity to write it down.

Ex: My name is Joseph with Company ABC ...

13. State your slogan or tagline.

    Leave a lasting impression – refine your tagline to ensure it's captivating and has a catchy and lasting impression – just like you!

    Ex: My name is Joseph with Company ABC, bringing the treasures of the earth to the people of the world through coffee.

Here is my entire 60-second elevator speech (also available in the Appendix for easy reference):

"Good morning/afternoon/evening, I am Joseph Luckett with Company ABC. We created the world's first nutritional, acid-free coffee. When you have regular coffee of any kind, it can cause acid reflux, jitters, shakes, and crashes, but one cup of our coffee contains the following nutrients per cup: 150 antioxidants, 200 vitamins and minerals, 800 times more vitamin B2 than Kiwi, three times more protein than peanut butter, three times more antioxidants than blueberries, and more. We focus on residential and commercial clients using our model called 'free-sample marketing,' which allows the potential user to try before buying. This month, I would love an email introduction to the following three professions: lawyers, restaurant owners, and salon owners in St. Louis, Chicago, and New York. From an individual perspective, I would love to be introduced to John Smith, Owner of XYZ Business. Thank you, So-and-So, for inviting me to this group. My name is Joseph with Company ABC, bringing the treasures of the earth to the people of the world through one-of-a-kind coffee."

The elevator speech is also where you reveal your specific call to action to a group of people. This is where you lay the groundwork for who you would like to meet. You should change up which industry you're looking for each week in a regularly scheduled group and make it event-specific if you're attending a professional group, like a manufacturers' group or an IT group. There are 84 different industries (see industry chart in Appendix). The more quality relationships you have across industries, the more valuable your network becomes. It's also wise to mix up your speech when you're frequently delivering it to the same people. The ultimate goal is to keep it fresh and full of energy so you can leave an impression.

I learned the importance of a great elevator speech by watching good commercials. Good commercials can drive business, just as bad commercials can lose business. The same principle applies in networking with the way your elevator speech resonates – and I've witnessed this in action. I've watched people deliver killer elevator speeches and build massive businesses and I've watched individuals deliver weak elevator speeches while their businesses struggled. I've observed and been a witness to the correlation between clear communication about my own business and the growth of that business. Within a group, there will be questions that need to be answered about your business. How well and how quickly you can clearly answer those questions directly correlates to the introductions and referrals you will receive.

Write out your elevator speech, practice it out loud, practice with your loved ones, time it, and get it just right. That way, when you're in a room full of people, you'll be less likely to falter and your confidence will shine.

Four Types of Elevator Speeches

Now that you know how to give your speech, you should know about the four types of elevator speeches you may hear from others, so you can understand just how important it is to master yours. You will also gain an understanding of the personalities associated with each type of elevator speech and what to avoid on your own. The benefit in learning the types of elevator speeches is twofold. First, it will help you be most efficient with your time, and second, you'll get a sense of people's personality types. When you understand someone's personality, you can better tender the pitch for your product or service and maximize your overall efforts in the meeting. When you understand people, you deepen your relationships, and that leads to the best form of networking and connecting – reciprocity. **Once you've reached the state of reciprocity, you can maximize your networking efforts.**

Here are four of the most familiar types of elevator speeches:

1. The Conference Goer's Elevator Speech

- Typically delivered by an individual who just returned from a business-related event or trip and all they talk about are the highlights of the trip.
- This person is excited to talk about the trip because it's what's most relevant at the moment, or because this individual is overly anxious about their needs.
- The content is often about things that benefit this individual rather than things that would benefit everyone in the room.

The elevator speech is not the right time to talk about a recent conference or something upcoming that's new and exciting for you. The time for those comments is at the end of the meeting. The elevator speech is your commercial not an update on your life.

The Conference Goer also tends to be the bottom-feeder type of networker. This person often only has their own interests in mind, as reflected by the content of the elevator speech. Whether it's truly due to selfish intentions or simply because the Conference Goer is ill-informed, there is some work to be done to make this elevator speech more appealing to everyone in the room.

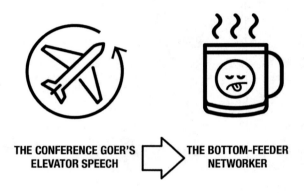

THE CONFERENCE GOER'S ELEVATOR SPEECH → **THE BOTTOM-FEEDER NETWORKER**

I've heard many Conference Goers' elevator speeches at networking events. They're usually full of the person's company lingo, company culture, and promo deals, and lack focus and value. I've found many network marketers, in particular, struggle with this. The solution? **Tweak the content of your speech to focus on the value your business delivers. This makes it less self-focused and more others-focused.**

2. The Politician's Elevator Speech

- Used as a platform to share views, thoughts, and solutions on an issue this person is passionate about.
- Sounds more like a political speech.
- Instead of having a call to action that provides some value, it's an invitation for others to join in the crusade.

The Politician tends to also be the hobbyist-type of a networker. This person generally networks for a social cause or simply just to be social, so the call to action in this elevator speech can be political and/or off-putting because it's unrelated to business.

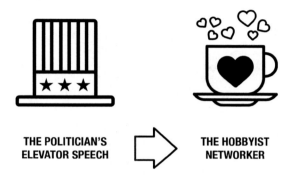

THE POLITICIAN'S
ELEVATOR SPEECH

THE HOBBYIST
NETWORKER

You will often hear the Politician's elevator speech when something happens on the news and they feel compelled to take a stance on an issue when given a platform. For example, I heard one of these speeches after a "Build the Wall" headline came up in the news. There is a place for talking about public issues in networking, but your elevator speech is not the time to soapbox – it's a time for promoting your business through a proposition of value. Follow my elevator speech blueprint to refocus your message from political to promotional.

3. The Confusing Elevator Speech

Very lengthy and rambly – the 60-second elevator speech is delivered in two or more minutes and by the time it's finished, you're wildly confused as to what this person does.

This person might even get a little greedy with having the platform and try to speak about other business ventures.

Some might even throw in a nonprofit or charity to confuse you even more.

Confusers are almost always serial networkers. They do not have a consistent call to action because they have so many different business ventures.

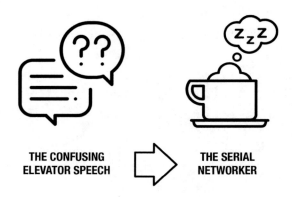

THE CONFUSING ELEVATOR SPEECH → **THE SERIAL NETWORKER**

Confusing elevator speeches always leave me uncertain of how to refer to the person who delivered the speech. Most of the time, the Confuser will jump from topic to topic and make it difficult to understand their message. Here's a tip — if you're worried your elevator speech might confuse people, call someone who heard it two weeks earlier and ask that person to explain back to you what you do. If they can't recall what you do, then it's time to revisit the clarity of your elevator speech.

4. The On-Point Elevator Speech

- A great 60-second commercial that stays within the time limit.
- You will know exactly who this person is and what their company is about with great clarity, but you will be left not knowing what type of introduction or referral they would prefer.
- Lacks a networking call to action.

Those who deliver an On-Point elevator speech are often new networkers who are evaluating what connections work best for them. Because newbie networkers are in the process of figuring out who they want to be connected to, they may leave out or be unclear about who they're looking for.

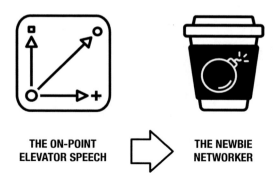

THE ON-POINT ELEVATOR SPEECH ➡ **THE NEWBIE NETWORKER**

I have found that On-Point elevator speeches capture my attention well, and when the person leaves out who they want to connect with, it's an opportunity for me to learn more about this individual. We set up a one-on-one meeting, and at that time, I gain clarity about who they are looking for. However, not everyone is willing to take this approach, so if your speech lacks a call to action, I recommend honing your target market so you can plug it into your elevator speech. Even if your target changes over time as you hone your ideal referral, you'll meet a lot of people along the way who can help you get to your goal while you help them in return.

5. The Example Elevator Speech
- Incredibly intentional – the type of elevator speech every person should aim to give.
- A wonderful commercial plus a precise idea of who the person is looking for in an introduction or referral.
- Typically, very specific about introductions/referrals – down to the city, state, county, province, country, and industry.
- Leaves a lasting impression of the person and their company.
- You can't wait to set up a meeting; you're left wanting to know more!

The Example elevator speech is often delivered by connector-types of networkers. These people have refined their ideal connections and know exactly what to say to get the right referral or introduction. Find my elevator speech in the Appendix to serve as an example for you.

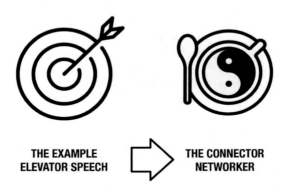

THE EXAMPLE
ELEVATOR SPEECH

THE CONNECTOR
NETWORKER

When I hear an Example elevator speech, it not only leaves me wanting to make introductions or referrals for a person – it encourages *everyone in the room* to provide introductions and referrals for exactly who this connector is seeking to meet. These speech givers receive referrals at scale, and regularly bring guests to events so they have the opportunity to make introductions to their guests.

The ability to identify the types of elevator speeches and who gives them will make you more aware of what people are saying at networking events and help guide you when refining your elevator speech so you can attract more business.

Bringing it Back to Coffee

To help understand the unique flavor and depth you bring to the networking world, you have to ferment and refine your elevator speech so people know exactly who you are, what you offer, and what kind of connections will grow your business.

To craft or re-craft your elevator speech, use the elevator speech blueprint in this chapter. Then sign up to join the Zero

to 100™ Platform once completed for future opportunities to practice delivering your elevator speech: https://zeroto100.io/

CHAPTER 5

Grading the Beans

The Follow Up

Once coffee beans have been pulped, fermented, and dried, there are still layers of the beans that need to be removed to refine their quality. What's left after the layers are removed and the bean is polished and graded, are the beans without defect that move through to the next stage. In networking, your elevator speech helps you peel back your own layers and leave those first impressions, which are, in effect, 'graded.' Then the impressions without 'defect' move through to the next stage, where you receive introductions and referrals. Here's where the best beans end up as great coffee – following up with those intros and/or referrals in an efficient, reliable manner.

This chapter will help you be diligent with your after-networking follow up and scheduling to stay focused and on the right track. You will learn how to follow up in the most methodical way by breaking down your business card collection and categorizing it by territory to best fit your schedule, as well as the most efficient process for scheduling effective meetings around your availability. **We make time for what is important to us, regardless of our schedule, and we must treat our connections with importance by managing our time effectively.**

Busyness vs. Productivity

Okay, so you've been to a networking event, you are now in the driver's seat. You have met quite a few people and made some deeper connections, now you need to schedule Caffeinated Moments to learn more about them and their businesses. This is the place where most people fail and lose their credibility. You may have made an amazing impression and promised to reach out and connect with at least one person, however, like many others, you find the hardest thing to do is to actually follow up and set that appointment. Do you feel you are too busy to make time to connect on an individual basis? What if the person you're "too busy to meet with" could be your next client, customer, or referral partner?

First of all, we are never too busy to do something that we place value in. **There is a fine line between being busy and being productive. The difference comes down to efficiency.** *Busyness* can mean you are very disorganized with your time and potentially spreading yourself too thin. You will find busy people fall into this trap of busyness by their own hand as it's difficult for them to say no. Learning how to say "no" will keep you organized and on track – especially if structure is not one of your strong suits.

When your plate is too full, the ball gets dropped often. For example, a person once booked a meeting with me and ended up going to the wrong coffee shop in a completely different part of town. This person was spread so thin that they were forgetting where meetings were booked. Some might fall into this category of "busy" and come across as not very focused. They appear quite focused during the conversation in and around events, but when it comes to the follow-up stage, the unfocused networker will emerge. These folks tend to cancel or reschedule appointments because they forget about prior engagements or perhaps cut your meeting short because of an overbooked time slot.

In the context of virtual networking when you aren't able to network in person, people's priorities shift. Networking becomes a necessity, but it can also be fatiguing. A person who had been wanting to meet with me for over a year but hadn't yet due to scheduling conflicts decided they didn't want to meet me anymore after the pandemic started. They told me they specifically wanted the experience of meeting me in person and because I decided to network nearly exclusively in a virtual setting during the pandemic, that wasn't an option, so we didn't meet at all. This individual also told me that they froze their membership to a networking group because they felt like people weren't as engaged as they should be in the virtual setting and it was challenging getting to know people. This is a valid sentiment to have around virtual networking, particularly when it's the only option. When you're forced to network in a way that limits the full picture of a person, it can be exhausting and discouraging. However, by giving up on meeting with a person altogether, you can miss out on opportunities to grow your business. That's why it's wise to keep your membership with networking groups and reap the value of connecting one-on-one, even if it is virtual – because there's so much potential for business growth when you commit yourself to build deeper REAL-ationships with individuals who are part of the same group. One-on-one meetings are what build and sustain an organization, provide more opportunities for members, create REAL-ationships, and grow revenue for an entire organization.

If you do decide to freeze your membership, do the following so that you can continuously add value to the organization and keep the opportunity, company, mission, and vision alive for current and future members while you're on that networking group hiatus.

- Set a tentative date for reinstating your membership so that the owner can hold you accountable, you can hold yourself accountable, and thus take your REAL-ationship to a different level

- Send the owner of the networking group a personal message and, if you're comfortable, let them know why you're freezing your membership. This provides them insight into how they can provide better value for current and future members.
- Ask the owner how you can continue to add value to the group.
- Find ways to actively promote the group to others while you're on hiatus to help get guests to attend meetings. This creates more opportunities for members and allows the group to sustain.
- Continue scheduling one-to-ones (Caffeinated Moments) with members of the group to keep building REAL-ationships.

Note: Networkers are constantly pivoting and adapting. Hybrid networking is a combination of face-to-face networking and virtual networking. This kind of networking allows you to meet with people locally in person but also connect with people from all over the world through virtual means.

My advice is to harmonize your schedule to ensure you're open to opportunities and manage your networking meetings without getting overwhelmed. Get into the habit of saying, "Now is not a good time, but can I connect with you _____?" and fill in the blank with a time that works for you. Book meetings as far out as possible if your schedule is full. When someone makes the effort to meet with you, it is always a good idea to show them that you are appreciative.

A productive person understands the power of saying no and the right time to do so.

Being productive happens when you're organized and respectful of your time and others' time. Productivity is working *in* the business. Busyness is working *on* the business.

Categorize Your Business Cards/Contacts

Many people will network and forget they have 100 business cards back at the office or at home that they've likely never followed up on because they're too busy pursuing new business cards or contact information. If the business cards you collect don't go anywhere, then what's the point of collecting them? Networking won't grow your business unless you have a follow-up process in place to handle business cards/contact information and start REAL-ationship building.

While there's plenty of technology out there to help you categorize business cards, I initially chose to categorize business cards manually. You're welcome to draw inspiration from my system or create your own system. Here's what I do … first, to effectively schedule meetings, I categorize my most recent collection of business cards and start categorizing them based on location. I start with the general location (country or state), then break down the categories into more specific locations (cities and towns). I begin by scheduling the closest city or town, then further break down the cards in each city/town by industry.

Finally, I further break down the industries in each city/town by people's culture. This is so that when I schedule meetings, I set them up intending to introduce people of different cultures to one another as they're crossing paths to meet with me. This is how I help fulfill my connections' cultural wheelhouses, and you can too. This is also possible to do virtually. (This will be discussed later on in Chapter 6). Remember – there are multiple ways to organize your business cards, but to be most effective with your time and scheduling meetings over coffee, you need to find an organizational method that suits you.

Note: It's one thing to collect everyone's business cards. If you'd like to have all your contacts consolidated into a digital format, we have a resource for you. ALLinEntry is able to convert all your contacts into one clean spreadsheet, so you build the list that builds your business. This is the next best step and it allows you to get past the obstacles and excuses of data entry that cost you time and money. Visit: www.allinentry.com/Zeroto100

Categorize Your Phone Contacts

We all love our cell phones for many reasons but did you know, they are a great tool for organizing contacts so you can find people fast and make referrals with light speed? If you're like most of us, you put contacts in your phone the traditional way with first and last name and company. Maybe you log everyone a different way or often can't remember a contact's last name on the spot. This can lead to a struggle when you need to find a person's contact info because you don't have an easy system to access it quickly. The fix: set up your phone with different industry categories like Chiropractors, Realtors, Lawyers, Life Coaches, etc., then add your contacts under those categories. As you meet people and get their names (ask if they prefer a shortened version and add that too; for example, does Steven like to be called Steve?), business cards, social media handles, phone numbers, email addresses, and any other pertinent information, you simply add them to their industry category. You can also create a code for where you met each person and add it after their name, like B for BNI or CC for the Chamber of Commerce. Your entire networking experience just became super efficient! At your next Hot Coffee meeting, when your contact asks for an introduction to a chiropractor, go to that industry on your phone and make as many chiropractor introductions as the person can handle. You can even take a screenshot of your list and text it, just be sure you let those contacts know your connection will be contacting them. No cold coffee here!

Note: Make it a priority to collect not only business email addresses and phone numbers but also personal emails and phone numbers. If the pandemic taught us anything, it's that jobs can easily change and it's easy to lose touch with people if you're not intentional enough about connecting with the person and not just the business they represent. To build a REAL-ationship, you need personal information——not just business information.

Continue to Add Contacts in the Same Industry

Now that you've organized your contacts, have you found 10 chiropractors, 25 insurance agents, and 40 real estate agents? That's great! Keep them all. It is important to continue to add more of the staple industries to your contact list and never really stop. When it comes to many industries, the failure rate is very high. If you have multiples in your wheelhouse to refer/introduce, you won't lose out. According to BizMiner, of the 1,021,350 general contractors and operative builders, heavy construction contractors, and special trade contractors operating in 2014, only 722,281 were still in business in 2016. This is a 29.3% failure rate. Other industry failure rates include real estate agents at 87%, insurance agents at 90%, and financial advisors at 88%. So keep your list full and edit it as needed.

Scheduling Meetings

Now it's time to book meetings that best fit your schedule. A methodical process for scheduling meetings effectively manages your time based on your availability. Whether you have four days available per week to meet or only one, **schedule your time effectively.** This brings the most value to the people you network with, develops you as a great connector, and also avoids the issue of becoming energetically drained by too much networking.

I spend 729 hours a year networking. That's 64 hours each month or 16 hours a week. I realize this is a lot more networking than most people have time for, and people ask me how I manage to network as much as I do while also being productive with my work. The secret is block scheduling, or "stack days." Stack days are multiple meetings set up back-to-back at one location. Mondays, Tuesdays, and Thursdays are my networking days. I have four hour-long periods blocked out on each of those days, with thirty minutes scheduled between each meeting. This 30-minute period is used either as a meeting overlap to introduce people to one another or to collect myself for my next meeting. Wednesdays are my administrative days, or my follow-up days – this is my dedicated time to make referrals and introductions and respond to emails, texts, voicemails, and messages. Friday is my Zero to 100™ day where I focus solely on the business. Saturdays and Sundays I have off.

Time	Mon	Tue	Wed	Thu	Fri	Sat	Sun
9:30 AM							
10:00 AM	Networking Meeting	Networking Meeting		Networking Meeting			
10:30 AM							
11:00 AM							
11:30 AM	Networking Meeting	Networking Meeting		Networking Meeting			
12:00 PM			Admin Day		Zero-To-100 Business		
12:30 PM							
1:00 PM	Networking Meeting	Networking Meeting		Networking Meeting			
1:30 PM							
2:00 PM							
2:30 PM	Networking Meeting	Networking Meeting		Networking Meeting			
3:00 PM							

Stack days are not a new development and are extremely effective for those with a limited amount of time. This especially benefits those with tight schedules who can only get away for a few hours or those with limited travel capabilities. When you utilize stack days for the benefit of others, you create an undeniable value. Being focused on one location alleviates the rush and allows effective connecting to happen. Scheduling stack days virtually is even easier (as long as your internet connection is stable) because there's no need to commute and the risk of running late is reduced.

When you schedule stack days it's important to know a little about who you're meeting with so you can schedule overlaps for each meeting to facilitate meet-and-greets. When you schedule two back-to-back meetings – one that ends at 1 p.m. and one that begins at 1 p.m. – you provide overlap time for these folks to meet each other. As the first meeting nears closing, be attentive to when the second person walks in so you can bring them over to meet the first person. If you're meeting virtually, you can easily overlap the meetings by providing your guests with the same video URL link. Begin to wrap up your meeting toward the last 10-15 minutes of the time you've scheduled so you will have ample time to begin edifying your next meeting. Ask each guest for enough business cards to share with the rest of your meetings that day (or to pull up their digital business card or contact information on the shared screen if it's a virtual meeting) and be sure to share your intent to talk about them in your remaining meetings. This creates a buzz for each meeting and shows your value as a great connector. When stacking, share tidbits about the next person so the current person knows who you are connecting them to. I often encourage people to take notes on the back of the business cards or in a journal dedicated to networking and tell them to build on that information. This creates some hype, and as your next guest arrives, you can motion for them to come over for an introduction to your current guest. The next guest can then grab something to drink or eat as you finish up the previous meeting. When you sit down with the next person, you can explain why you're connecting the two of them and suggest they schedule a meeting. Hopefully, by the end of each meeting, your guests will be motivated to reach out to the six or seven intro-ductions you arranged in passing.

In the end, each of your new contacts will have met the same number of people you met with that day. So if you have eight meet-ings that day, you get seven business cards from Person 1 and explain who you're meeting with later. Each subsequent person you meet with will get seven introductions! The first person will get the list of the day's cards emailed to them (as you won't have any yet at the first meeting), and the last person's information will be emailed to everyone you met with that day (as this is your last person, there are no subsequent introductions to give cards to). Arranging connec-tions like this makes you a valuable person that everybody wants to meet with because you can introduce them to even more people. Another great benefit to well-executed stack days with introduc-tions is the value you bring to other networking groups. The person you met with will go into their other weekly meetings and share with the group how amazing your meeting was and how great it was to be introduced to so many others with a warm introduction. This creates buzz around you and drums up the curiosity to meet with you.

However, you decide to schedule your meetings, being method-ical about it is the best way to manage your time and stay consid-erate of those you meet without getting burned out. Consider this: the *quality* of connections created in networking happens through intentionality – intentionality can only come from a well-balanced, or what I like to call, a "harmonized" and organized scheduling process.

Study Results: How Participants Maintained Their Network

Participants in the study used a broad range of platforms to main-tain their network.

- 74% used Social Media

- 74% used In-Person Meetings
- 64% used email
- 56% used Text Messages
- 31% used Telephone Calls

The platforms participants used to maintain their network did not affect how strongly their networking and business benefited from Zero to 100™, again, the improvements were always based on how closely they followed the principles within the book.

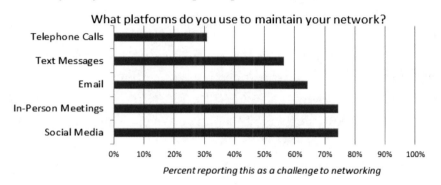

What platforms do you use to maintain your network?

Percent reporting this as a challenge to networking

Participants responded that they spent approximately 10-20 minutes per day maintaining their network. This was consistent throughout the study.

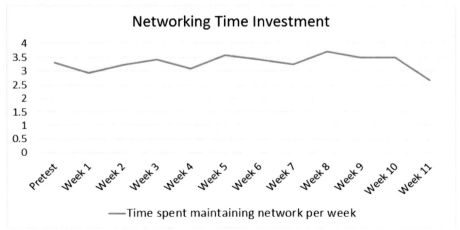

Networking Time Investment

Time spent maintaining network per week

Maintaining your network is even more doable in a virtual setting because people are more willing than before to open up as we have the shared experience of a life-changing pandemic. Icebreakers come easier than before. When you're thinking of a person, simply send them a message with whatever mode of communication you're comfortable with and ask how they're doing. You can even include a photo of you with this person (if you have one) which communicates "I haven't forgotten about you." If you're limited to virtual follow-ups only, be sure to switch up your mode of communication to keep it fresh.

My friend Kimberly Ferguson shared her thoughts with me on how virtual networking enhanced her connections through the 2020 pandemic: "I find myself able to be much more intentional about virtual networking. Instead of meeting up every six months or a year., I check in with people more often via Facebook, text message, or phone call. I have to think about and plan times to check in with people, as I don't see them out and about anymore. I think it's been a really good shift that I plan to continue even as things return to in-person networking."

Bringing it Back to Coffee

Just like grading coffee beans, refining the quality of your follow-up process will yield the most effective networking and therefore, the best cup of coffee and optimum results. You'll get high-quality meetings with a grading process that works for you.

CHAPTER 6

Roasting & Grinding the Beans
Meetings Over Coffee

Green coffee beans are roasted over 400°F (204°C). Different durations of roasting result in different flavors and characteristics. Freshly roasted beans set you up perfectly for finely ground coffee. Grinding takes time and effort but it's necessary for reaping the rewards of the bean. Your meetings over coffee in networking are the same way – you have to put the work in to build relationships by asking questions that give you a steaming hot cup of business. If there's no grinding, there's no business. Just as with the roasting process, each of your meetings over coffee will have different flavors and characteristics. And as with the grinding of coffee, your efforts to build off of those flavors and characteristics over time will form REAL-ationships that yield quality referrals and/or introductions.

In this chapter, I'll explain what I call the Coffee Shop Experience – or how I set the tone for every meeting with connetiquette and respect to leave a favorable impression. I break down how to have efficient Meetings Over Coffee where you'll have the opportunity to use the Caffeinated Moment and its counterpart, the "What's Your Story?" Questionnaire. You can use both of these tools to guide you as a driver and a passenger in each meeting. Lastly, we'll dive into what it means to have "Hot Coffee," or in other words, the power of creating strong connections.

The Coffee Shop Experience

I try to give every person I sit down with the "Coffee Shop Experience," meaning that I treat every person as my guest and want to make him or her feel comfortable in our meeting. Oftentimes, traditional "one-to-one meetings" are associated with pushing a sale, so people come into these meetings uncomfortable, with the anticipation that you might just be trying to sell them something. The only time someone rushes you in a meeting is when they want to sell to you, and that same kind of person isn't interested in meeting with you more than once. The Coffee Shop Experience and the Caffeinated Moment are all about dumping the notion that Meetings Over Coffee are about pushing sales – **these meetings have one simple purpose: to get to know one another.**

A local business person reached out to me on Facebook to schedule a meeting, and when we got together, this person brought two other people to the meeting without telling me they were coming. They spent most of the meeting pitching to me. I finally said to my original connection, "You're operating from a transactional mindset. You have three people sitting at this table; do you think we can actually learn from each other?" After that, one of the others changed the way she was networking. This person is now a friend of mine and a great networker. But two of these people missed out on networking opportunities in that meeting because the one who scheduled it got greedy about using the time to solely promote their business. There was no intention of getting to know me nor was I able to learn more about this individual. The possibility of connecting and having a Caffeinated Moment was squandered.

The Virtual Coffee Shop Experience

It's important to note that you can (and should) provide the Coffee Shop Experience anywhere, regardless of location or if the meeting is face-to-face or virtual. In the virtual setting, the Coffee Shop Experience means:

1. A stable internet connection.

2. Good lighting (it makes a huge difference!).

3. Coming to the meeting prepared, having gone through a tutorial, and practicing your video platform of choice if you are new to virtual networking via video. Understand how to use the platform features such as the chatbox, Screen Share, "Raise Your Hand" features, etc. These features are important for getting the most out of communicating.

4. Checking in prior to the meeting to make sure that the person you're meeting knows how to use whatever virtual platform you're using, knows the meeting code if there is one, knows how to use the Screen Share function, etc.

5. Testing audio and video 5 to 10 minutes before the call to ensure tech is running smoothly.

6. Using headphones in a quiet, private space to optimize sound quality on both ends of the call.

7. Limiting visual distractions by using a plain and calm background. Avoid using virtual backgrounds because they make the body look choppy and can distract from people being able to focus on what you're saying when you speak.

8. Using Screen Share to exchange virtual business cards or any contact information of introductions and referrals.

Networking is about building relationships, and building relationships takes time. So settle in and aim to make every meeting a consistently excellent experience for whoever sits across from you. Also note that, regardless of the meeting setting, whatever you don't cover in a meeting with someone gives you another reason to get back together again. From pre-arrival to saying goodbye, use your *connetiquette* – the etiquette that should take place while connecting.

Connetiquette

Before you sit down at your meeting, be it your first or hundredth, you must reflect on your connecting etiquette, or *connetiquette.* When making your first impression, you want to be remembered – **so be remembered for the way you respected your guest from the very start to the end of your meeting and all the times you connect thereafter.**

- L, H, & E – Listen, hear, and engage.
- Be interested, not interesting (self-absorbed).
- Have your business card where it can be seen first before giving it to someone (or sharing it with them virtually via Screen Share before the meeting has even started), never be slick and shake someone's hand with it or neglect to explain why you're sharing it digitally.
- Respect people's time – always! In networking events, during the Caffeinated Moment, on phone calls, your 60-, 45-, 30-second elevator speech, presentations, etc.
- Praise in public, coach in private. If a person could be more efficient in an area but may not know it, tell them in private, because at the end of the day, it's about the marathon and the North Star of networking, which is the REAL-ationship.
- Respect everyone at an event or in any networking setting by not being on your phone or looking at it all the time. Better yet, silence it and put it away while you're networking. Similarly, in

a virtual setting, be sure to minimize other windows and digital distractions on your computer.

- Take virtual meetings on a computer rather than a phone if you can because notifications from the phone can be distracting and even interrupt the meeting altogether.
- Also, talking to your neighbor when someone is speaking shoots your likeability in an instant.
- Do not, after a networking event or meeting, *automatically* add people to your email blasts, newsletter program, or text messaging system. Always ask first.
- Similarly, after you meet with someone and add them on Facebook with their permission, don't automatically send them a request to like your fan or business page unless you have asked. This can be a real turn-off and you get lumped in with those annoying auto-senders.
- Do not make it an "I" thing, make it a "we" thing in every facet of networking.
- Do not set up a Caffeinated Moment with someone and try to date or hit on him or her.
- Always be in the mode/mindset of serving.

Take Notes. In meetings, it's helpful to take notes so that you truly follow through with what you say and can remember essential details. How many of us remember, after a few meetings, who we promised to make an introduction to? Which referrals to send, who to follow up with, and about what? Then there's remembering to attend an event that someone has invited you to, and great new tips, strategies, and tactics that you might miss out on if you don't take notes. Do it however it makes sense to you, but I find writing on paper (the old fashioned way) helps me stay focused on the person in front of me without having to constantly look down to type on a phone, tablet, or laptop. This could also be misinterpreted as you texting someone else or being distracted, which comes off as rude. Also, it's impossible to give your full attention and take notes when you're eating, so if you're at a place that serves food, be sure to have eaten before your meeting. At the risk of repeating myself, I am going to say it again – there's so much to miss out on if you do not take notes.

Hygiene. Living through pandemic and post-pandemic times means that in-person meetings require a level of hygiene that was not expected before. This means wearing a mask and socially distancing when possible – and it may not be the expectation in perpetuity, but it is important to be respectful of this expectation as we slowly transition back to something resembling normalcy pre-COVID. I wear a mask for the same reason I give you introductions and referrals: I care about you. Also, it should go without saying, but the world has gotten so lax in personal hygiene and presentation, that it gets easier and easier to show up without taking care of your appearance. Therefore, I must say it – look professional! How you appear to others speaks volumes about how you feel about yourself. I can't tell you how many times I've either met with someone who looks like they just climbed out of bed or watched others at my meeting places show up to meet people for the first time disheveled and unclean, hair a mess, stained clothes, in baggy t-shirts and what look like pajama bottoms. Pull yourself together. Wash yourself. Get rid of the bad breath (even if you have to chew gum) or discreetly offer the other person a breath mint as you get one for yourself. Comb your hair, shine or wipe off your shoes, iron your clothes, get the crust out of your eyes, and wash your hands if you're a sweaty person or if you've just come from outside. Bottom line: get yourself together – please! When you show up professionally groomed, you show respect for yourself and the other person. You should be doing this in virtual meetings too, especially since you don't even have to look professional from the waist down!

Respect Time. I mention this often, but I simply cannot stress this fact enough. Respecting people's time is critical to being liked and building meaningful REAL-ationships. Regardless if you were the person who booked the meeting or the person who accepted the meeting, it's imperative that you arrive early, well-groomed, and not frazzled. Arriving early for a meeting is a great sign of respect. It shows that your guest is important to you and that you value their time. This will also give you time to gather yourself mentally and set up all the necessary tools to learn about the person you're meeting (pen, paper, laptop, etc.), especially if you have been on the move since the start of your day. In a virtual setting, you need to take extra care to come prepared to ensure you can have a meeting that starts on time and has minimal interruptions or delays due to tech or connectivity issues.

When you schedule yourself too thin, your guest will pick up on your rushing and stressed mannerisms. Arriving early allows enough time to scan the room to see if there are any acquaintances, clients, customers, or referral partners in the area who might be great introductions or referrals for your guest. An extra 15 to 20 minutes to visit with your associates prepares your motor skills and fires you up so you're primed to provide the utmost value throughout your meetings. Some of us struggle with time management when we're juggling working in our business and networking for our business, and both are important activities. By taking these extra steps, you'll be better prepared for each meeting, which is priceless to your networking success and business.

Prepare. There are several things you can do prior to each meeting that will eliminate distractions and provide a comfortable environment for your guests…

- Before the meeting, select an appropriate table to create a great working atmosphere. You should have ample room on the table for notetaking and beverages, in addition to being away from the majority of foot traffic – this will eliminate most distractions and passerbys.
- Make sure to take a moment to wipe down your table and chairs – keeping the space disinfected is safe and considerate, plus, some people are very particular and can easily be distracted by crumbs. This will also save him or her from having to clean it and taking valuable time away from the meeting.
- Another courteous gesture for an in-person meeting is to call or text ahead and ask if your guest would like anything. Having their request waiting at the table upon arrival is a considerate way to show thanks for that person's time.
- Lead with permission – send a message to whoever you're meeting with beforehand and ask if there are things they would like you to keep in mind in the context of health and safety in the pandemic so they can be comfortable during the meeting. Ask what greeting they would prefer (handshake, elbow bump, foot tap, etc.).
- Prepare your virtual environment by ensuring your space is clean, presentable, and has no distractions.

Upon your guest's arrival, walk over and greet him or her at the door with a little small talk about the day. Pulling out their chair is a kind and hospitable gesture, regardless of gender, and sets the tone for an amazing meeting. You can also place your guest in the chair that backs to the foot traffic, creating an environment for a more focused meeting. Connetiquette.

Over the course of my experience in networking, you can bet I've had a lot of interesting Meetings Over Coffee – both absolutely fantastic meetings and not so great meetings. I have had some bad Coffee Shop Experiences, despite efforts to give my guests great experiences. For example, I once met a new connection, who was introduced to me via email, at a St. Louis Bread Company. I introduced this individual to two people I knew in the restaurant, then we sat down, I took out my pen and notebook, and we proceeded to have an awesome meeting. In the end, my new connection commented that the meeting was enjoyable. This person was impressed with the name I had built for myself, then ended by saying, "but I don't do business with African Americans." Then they proceeded to try to snatch my notes from me. It was stunning how quickly that meeting turned from positive to negative. I later called the connection who introduced us and discovered that this person was no longer employed and was suffering from a mental disorder. It was clear this individual was not doing well at the time of our meeting, so I hold no hard feelings. But, this just shows that sometimes meetings can go sour despite efforts to give a great Coffee Shop Experience. It is typically not a reflection on you when this happens, as not all people are meant to connect. I'm happy to say, though, that the vast majority of my meetings go well, as reflected in the following testimonial.

"What an absolute delight it was for me to meet with Joseph. He is high-energy; a stickler for detail with deep compassion and concern for people. He is transparent – honest and open about himself, his goals, and his expectations. I like that. It can be challenging to find genuine people in this world. On top of all that, he seeks to be the giver in relationships, both personally and in business."

– Delores Martin, Mary Kay, Independent Beauty Consultant

However, you choose to create your Coffee Shop Experience, remember that first impressions matter in networking and you have to consistently treat everyone with respect and kindness. Use the

Connetiquette guide to offer your best self to others and watch your REAL-ationships expand with a genuine love for mutual connecting.

The Driver & The Passenger

In every meeting, it's important to determine who will start as the driver and who will start as the passenger. The driver will be the one who talks about himself or herself and their business first, answering questions posed by the passenger while the passenger takes notes and learns from the person speaking. Both of you should have equal time driving the meeting. Ideally, you want a balance so both of you have time to get to know one another and hopefully exchange some introductions at the end of the meeting. So, if you are in the driver's seat first, be mindful of your time and give your guest the opportunity to drive so they can ask questions about you! If you don't get through every question on the "What's Your Story?" Questionnaire (which I'll cover later in the chapter) or through every point on the Caffeinated Moment form within your allotted time frame, that's okay. This creates the perfect opportunity to schedule a second meeting, and in my opinion, that's where th relationship building really starts — in the second meeting.

There are two ways to drive the meeting. You can either drive into a ditch or down the highway. When you drive a person into the ditch of confusion, they will end up leaving the meeting unclear about what you do. Over-complicating your message or not answering all the questions asked makes for an ineffective meeting. So be sure to refine your elevator speech and/or your own Caffeinated Moment before the meeting. If your guest is new to networking, it's your role to drive the meeting. With a new networker, you have an opportunity to provide value in networking and potential guidance as your guest grows their network. If you play the roles properly, you will have a high-value meeting.

When the driver and passenger roles aren't played properly, you end up with someone being too much of a driver or too much of a passenger, and the potential for connecting falls flat. I once met a person at Kaldi's Coffee who pitched their business and a bunch of different networking opportunities, and by the time they were finished pitching, there was no time left for me to talk. This person realized they monopolized the time, drove way too much of the meeting, and felt bad that I didn't have an opportunity to speak. I responded by saying it was okay, that I realized they were excited, and we could schedule a second meeting. I recommend practicing patience if you find someone drives too much of your meeting – give it a second shot to create that driver/passenger harmony.

There's also a good chance you'll sit down with someone who spends too much time as the passenger. This may be because a person is new to networking or shy and unclear on the intentions and purpose behind a meeting. I once had two meetings in a row with an individual who asked to meet with me, but didn't provide any introductions or referrals. It seemed like this person just wanted to take me on a business date and get together without the intent of creating introductions or referrals. When I asked about their intentions for our meetings, this individual apologized and admitted they didn't know how to make an introduction. I shared my method of setting up introductions and now this person is one of my strongest referral partners who even tries to outdo me in the number of introductions every time we meet!

When it's your turn to be the passenger in a meeting, you must know what questions to ask to make the most of your time. This is an opportunity to learn about each other, both on a personal and professional level. By learning something personal in your meeting, you get a better idea of who might be a good referral based on several factors like personality, values, lifestyle, and professional goals. Not everyone needs to or should do business with everyone, but you can always approach it with the intent to provide value. Do your best to understand who you are sitting with (or meeting with virtually) – pay attention to mannerisms and how questions are answered. Is your guest timid and quiet with one-word answers or does this person go on and on, excited to share their story? By adapting to their disposition – whether you need to turn your energy up or down as you go along – the other person will be more comfortable and open to share. This helps you know how to best refer or introduce others to this individual. When you go into each meeting with no judgments, you allow the conversation to flow organically. Be careful – if you've already researched the person on social media, you might walk into the meeting with preconceived opinions, which could potentially spoil the opportunity to learn directly from your guest. By asking a series of meaningful questions, you begin to peel back the layers and learn about someone so you can best introduce and refer the ideal clients or customers with the utmost benefit.

"What's Your Story?" Questionnaire

You get the most out of your meetings when you ask the right questions. The answers to these questions prime you to give the best introductions and referrals or they may change your mind about working with someone at all.

I created this abridged list of questions to help me become a successful referral partner and it works.

- What's the name of your business or company you work for? What do you do?
- How long have you been in business or with your company?
- How long have you been networking?
- Who introduced us?

- Where are you from?
- Do you have siblings? If so – are you close to them?
- Are you married? If so – how long, how did you meet, what does your spouse do?
- Do you have children? Do you have pets?
- Did you go to college? If so – where and what did you major in?
- Are you the first business owner/entrepreneur in your family?
- What market do you work in – residential or commercial?
- How do you get most of your sales?
- Are you involved in any networking groups? If so – which one(s)?
- Do you like to work on personal growth? If so – what's your preferred source (books, videos, podcasts, films, etc.) and favorite genre?
- Who would be a great introduction for you? Please be industry-specific*.
- Who would be a great referral for you? Please be industry-specific*.
- How many introductions can you handle per month? How would you like to receive these warm introductions?
- Do you work remotely?**
- Are you comfortable with meeting in person, virtually, or both?**
- What is/are your preferred virtual networking platform(s)?**

*You can find the complete list of industries in the Industry Wheelhouse section of the Appendix, along with a full version of the "What's Your Story?" Questionnaire with detailed explanations behind each question I ask in my meetings.

Now, I completely understand this questionnaire is not everyone's cup of tea (or coffee LOL) and information like whether or not someone has kids or likes to read may seem trivial or even inappropriate to some people. I once sat down with someone who reached out to me to set a meeting, and when we got to the "What's Your Story" Questionnaire, they didn't want to answer any of the personal questions about family, passions, or hobbies. This individual asked me why I wanted answers to these particular questions, and I said, "You can understand someone's professional life, but if you don't get to know their personality and what's important to that person, the relationship won't work."

The reason I use this questionnaire is that I've found it to be the easiest and most effective system in making referrals, introductions, and a faster-growing network of connections. It also helps me respect the time I have in the driver's seat, where I can share things about myself and my business most efficiently. That is also how I came up with the Caffeinated Moment, which you learned about back in Chapter 1.

When you're able to both *ask* the right questions and *answer* them, that's how you set yourself up for what I call **Hot Coffee.**

Hot Coffee Meetings

A "Hot Coffee Meeting" is the result of a powerful connection with a person with whom you meet consistently to exchange introductions and referrals. **This relationship is critical to becoming a connector and building a strong network.** I will dive into how to have a productive Hot Coffee Meeting in Chapter 7, but this is ultimately what you're working towards in your Meetings Over Coffee, and it's what will make all the networking worth it.

The "What's Your Story?" Questionnaire and Caffeinated Moment will help you to get the most out of your meetings and result in more introductions, referrals, clients, customers, and a faster-growing network of connectors. These tools will guide you to the right referral partners who then turn into Hot Coffee. The goal is a referral partnership where both parties agree to consistently pass quality introductions, referrals, and other connections back and forth in hopes of creating everlasting network growth and revenue.

Networking can be a very selfish sport. Connecting is a team-oriented sport.

Bringing it Back to Coffee

A Meeting Over Coffee that asks meaningful questions of the person across from you is a lot like roasting and grinding coffee beans to see what flavor and characteristics come out. REAL-ationship building takes time and effort, as does the perfect coffee bean, but it's worth the persistence and dedication for your business. There is a lot to be gained from this process.

CHAPTER 7

Brewing the Coffee
Tour Guide Networking

Brewing fresh coffee grounds is the final step before consuming your delicious coffee. This can take time and is very deliberate, but the rewards are well worth it – Tour Guide Networking is the same way.

Many people have asked how I was able to get my name on everyone's lips so quickly and across such diverse communities. The secret is the "Tour Guide" piece. When you take people on a guided tour of your specific introductions, there will be zero doubt as to who you would like to meet. **Tour Guide networking is essential to penetrate new networks and expand your network beyond your geographical location.**

You become a Tour Guide in Step #8 of the elevator speech blueprint. This is where you get super specific in requesting the introduction or referral that best fits your current needs. Not only should you mention the industry or industries you are most interested in doing business with, but also share specific names of individuals (if you have them) who would be great introductions or referrals within that community. The Tour Guide piece is used in multiple touchpoints of your networking:

1. Elevator Speech (Chapter 3)
2. The Introduction (Chapter 5)
3. The Caffeinated Moment (Chapter 1)
4. Meetings Over Coffee & Hot Coffee Meetings (Chapter 6)

If you recall from Chapter 3, the elevator speech is where you first reveal your specific introduction or referral request to a group of people. When you begin meeting with those new referrals, you should reiterate your ideal industry referral to each person to trigger their memory. Sometimes a connection will already have prepared a list of business owners within your wheelhouse to introduce you to. When you receive the introduction you've requested and set the meeting date, take the meeting in the community or city you are looking to reach if you are able. Since the pandemic, we have had to adapt our networking to include more virtual meetings – so now long-distance networking is not the only reason to meet virtually.

The importance of being as specific as possible cannot be stressed enough when Tour Guide Networking – you should name the city, state, or country, and the industry and/or the person with whom you'd like to connect. It is best if you have the name of a specific person you want to meet (but not necessary). This will give your guest a direct call to action to contact that person for a referral or check their network for your requested industry. If your guest is unfamiliar with the person you're asking to meet, they will most likely know of someone in that location who's willing to start the conversation for you.

Acting as a Tour Guide, I have been able to both create and receive great connections all over the United States and internationally. For example, I connected my content writer, Anya Overmann, to Juliet Bagwell who lives in St. Louis and wants to build a women and children's center in a remote part of Guatemala. Anya happens to know David, in Guatemala, who owns a construction company. She connected Juliet and David and a month after the introduction, Juliet flew to Guatemala, and the two met up to make plans for construction!

Juliet Bagwell and David Pineda in El Salitre, Guatemala

Similarly, my friend Carly Black acted as a Tour Guide to connect me with a woman in Massachusetts who runs a book club – now this book will be on her book list! Neither of these connections could have happened without Tour Guide networking.

To grow your network beyond your community, it's imperative that you also serve as a Tour Guide to share the value of your connections. In doing this, you're far more likely to see reciprocal introductions and referrals to people who could potentially catalyze the growth of your network in any given area. During your Meetings Over Coffee:

1. Ask for a tour of your connection's neighborhood network by using the F.O.R.M. technique – Friends/Family, Occupation, Recreation, and Message (see Chapter 2).

2. Then ask, "Who would you like to know in my city, across the U.S., or even the world?"

These questions create an opportunity for the other person to take a turn in the driver's seat.

You know people where you are from, even if you're new to networking, and have the chance to be the connector in your own backyard. It is a bonus if you know people outside of your geographical area that happens to fit your guest's ideal referral. And if you execute well as a Tour Guide, this creates an endless source of meetings, referrals, introductions, clients, and customers in whatever area you choose — hence the "tour."

Keys to Tour Guide Networking

1. When in a group function, during your elevator speech, share your specifications for introductions. Whether at an event or in a Caffeinated Moment, take the opportunity to share your vision and request specific introductions and/or referrals to the person who can potentially be the catalyst for you gaining traction in that area. It is important to serve as a Tour Guide for your community as well:

"I'm from _____ and I have a presence in _____ communities. Is there anyone you'd like to meet from there?"

2. When they answer your question about who in your city, across the U.S., or even the world that they would like to meet, send or receive email introductions to those people you think fit your connection's ideal referrals (email introduction template provided in Appendix).

3. When your connection provides referrals to you, schedule those meetings in your new referrals' communities — that's the point, to get out of your area and into theirs.

4. In your Meetings Over Coffee, restate that you're new to the community and looking for introductions there.

5. Ask if you can help expand your new connections' industries or cultural wheelhouses by making any introductions or referrals outside of their communities.

6. Schedule to meet every subsequent introduction you receive from that community within that geographical location.

Again, the pandemic changed life to make virtual networking more of a necessity, but we can continue Tour Guide Networking despite it. While nothing is the same as meeting face to face, powerful connections can still form virtually despite the distance. The potential to succeed through video and phone networking has never been stronger than it is today, and it's a reason to look forward to Tour Guide Reciprocity.

Tour Guide Reciprocity

You know your community and have the potential to be a connector in your backyard network. If done properly, Tour Guides will help grow your network outside of that backyard and you will assist in growing theirs within your community, resulting in **Tour Guide Reciprocity**. Once you successfully go through Tour Guide Reciprocity, you'll have deepened your REAL-ationship – which is the answer to a never-ending pool of introductions, referrals, and referral partners without geographical boundaries. Remember your elevator speech? The hard work of mastering that pays off here because you'll leave a lasting impression that intrigues others, compels them to learn more about you, and most importantly, those who are "wow'd!" by it will be excited to introduce you to their neighborhood network – then you can begin to build in any marketplace.

Mahatma Gandhi said it best, "If you don't ask, you don't get it." When you are looking to meet someone in a different area, **ask for the introduction or referral – you never know who someone might know.** There is this idea that all living things are six or fewer steps away from each other, so a chain of "a friend of a friend" can be made. Expanding your business across the world *is* possible and can happen when you ask for the right introduction or referral. When this is executed properly, it can take your business to new heights. But remember – **getting quality introductions and referrals starts with *giving* quality introductions and referrals** – in other words, you have to practice being a good Tour Guide.

Tips for Being a Good Tour Guide

- Toward the end of Meetings Over Coffee, ask people who they're looking to meet.
- Ask clarifying questions about the industry, location, personality, or even specific names so you can make the best considerations about people you know.
- Take notes – you won't always know how to best connect people off the top of your head, but when you write down who they're looking for, you can revisit and think more intently about who you might be able to introduce to one another.
- Offer to write a review, ask for a review – an online review on LinkedIn, Facebook, or Google adds value and credibility to a person or business, which in turn helps grow the business. This applies even more so in the remote landscape than ever before.

Being a good Tour Guide and giving freely encourages others to reciprocate and ultimately results in the growth of your network, your business, and your revenue stream.

Bringing it Back to Coffee

Tour Guide Networking takes time; it's a meticulous process, just like brewing coffee. The intentionality behind it creates high-quality, powerful connections. Brewing is a necessary part of the coffee-making process that requires patience, as does the growth of your networking through the Tour Guide process.

CHAPTER 8

Drinking Your Coffee

Working with "Hot Coffee" & How to Network On a Budget

The final and most delightful step in the coffee journey: consumption! "Drinking your coffee" in networking is the application of your REAL-ationships for personal and professional growth, which leads to success. Ultimately, the quality of what's in your cup depends on the journey the coffee bean has taken. Just like in networking, your best cups of coffee — or your best connections — come from the premium beans that have been grown, harvested, sorted, fermented, dried, pulped, graded, roasted, and ground to give you the best return. You've worked hard and efficiently to grow your harvest and brew those cups of Hot Coffee — now it's time to reap the benefits. This is the return on your networking investment (ROI), and in this chapter, you'll learn how to recognize and measure a successful ROI.

Along with guidance on how to budget for your networking in this chapter, I'll go over the concepts of "Hot Coffee" and "Mirror Matching."

Hot Coffee – Your Second Meeting

When you exchange introductions with someone after an initial meeting, it's time to set up a cup of Hot Coffee. **Hot Coffee meetings are when two people get together with the intent to grow one another's network and the revenue that results from cementing true reciprocity.** During or after your first meeting, let the person know that within 30, 60, or 90 days, you will get together for another meeting — a Hot Coffee meeting — with a list of new people to introduce to one another. Keep in mind, Hot Coffee only works if the first meeting goes well and you both leave with some introductions.

If you tap into Hot Coffee, no introductions will ever be cold. Every introduction to someone will be warm and guided by REAL-ationships. I am often asked, "How do you build a network at scale?" My reply is this: most people don't realize they can meet with the same person again and again to get a lot more value. In fact, you *need* to have multiple meetings with the same person because the better you get to know someone, the better you can refer to him or her and vice versa. People think successful networking is about being present at all the events and meetings, but it's not. What makes you successful is *not* being present everywhere but having your presence heard and felt everywhere anyway. I recommend a networking ratio of **50/50 – 50% repeat Hot Coffee meetings and 50% new people.**

Wondering how to set up Hot Coffee meetings? It is as easy as tapping into the stack of business cards (or contacts) you already have that are probably collecting dust and not making you any money. Contact these people – most likely you have already met each of them at least once to get their business card or contact information – and get them on your calendar. Out of 100 cards, you will probably get 20% to recommit to another meeting. The average person knows 200 people, so if you meet with 20 people and fully leverage those relationships, you have the potential to add 4,000 warm connections to your network. Spend your time building your database of virtual business cards. The objective in collecting that information is to get the best idea of what each person's business looks like.

Once you take a meeting with an existing contact, bring a list to the meeting with the number of new introductions and/or referrals you would like to share, and the other person will ideally do the same. You will make the connections, set a new meeting date, rinse and repeat. Over the course of a year, you can measure how many connections were made from each person and how much revenue was made as a result of those connections. Everybody wins.

A Few Meeting Arrangement & Follow-Up Tips

When you first reach out or have a meeting, make sure you have a follow-up activity planned. For instance, after your initial meeting, if you promise to make a referral, do so and keep a record of what you did, how, and when. If you call, leave a voicemail. Follow that up with an email, text, etc., and take notes about what you did to follow up. This ensures that when you run into a person who does not respond, you have peace of mind that you were not the one to drop the ball. We all know that life happens — phones lose data, things break, and messages get lost — but if you have a scheduled order with which to follow up, you know you have taken every opportunity to connect. Taking a little extra time to keep records of each attempt keeps you accountable.

This is what my follow-up process looks like. I do these in order until I get a response or schedule a meeting. Sometimes, I do a couple on the same day to the same person, sometimes I wait a day to go to the next one. It helps to know the person well enough to know if they typically take a day to respond or needs a couple of different attempts right away; don't hound him or her, but be diligent. If you don't know the person well, you may feel most comfortable reaching out with an email and maybe a text/IM first, then the next day, leave a voicemail. If still no response, try sending the email again a few days later with a kind note saying you want to be sure the email didn't end up in SPAM or get lost in the shuffle. This is how I follow up after every Caffeinated Moment meeting. You can find your own style, but stick to it for everyone, that way there's no confusion as to what you did with whom.

1. Call and leave a voicemail.

2. Send a Linkedin Message.

3. Send a Facebook Message.

4. Text Message.

5. Send an Email.

Once you get the person's attention, take a moment to schedule another meeting within six months from the one you just had, especially if you've had zero contact with this referral and/or introduction since your first meeting. This keeps the person from falling through the cracks and disappearing off of your radar. It is a great idea to keep a list of new referrals for your next meeting and make sure they know you have a list to share — this can inspire a meeting sooner rather than later and keep the connecting hot.

The next step in Hot Coffee is to take some time to reach out, right there in your meeting, and connect contacts with each other. Reference the list of new people you have met, along with your current contacts, and take five to ten minutes to set up each other's introductions via email, text, Facebook messenger, or a phone call. The goal is to make brand new introductions and/or referrals *during the meeting*. Always ask the person you are meeting with how many new referrals and/or introductions they can handle, then share away. The beauty of this process is that by the end of the day, you both could have responses from everyone who was introduced or referred to you during your meeting — which puts you both right to work!

The final ten minutes of your meeting should be dedicated to REAL-ationship building. Take time to get to know each other better. Learning more about someone and sharing experiences elevates the quality of referrals and/or introductions you send their way. **Remember — meaningful networking is all about quality, not quantity.** Getting to know someone with genuine interest shows through as you edify that person to others, and it opens doors to numerous opportunities for you both.

In your next meeting, repeat this process and give new introductions and/or referrals each subsequent time you meet. When this process is followed correctly, you create a trusted referral partnership where both parties achieve the coveted reciprocity. When maintained over the course of a year, the impact on each other's network, revenue, or both, will be clear and you'll have potentially created a new friendship!

Pro Tip: If you want to really impress the people you're introducing while also supplying them with incredible value, go for chained networking introductions. A chained networking introduction is where you add a list of all the connections (and their contact information) that led you to make the current introduction. Copying all of the people included on the list (with their permission) will alert those connections that they're receiving a new warm introduction.

Mirror Matching

Mirror matching, as first mentioned in Chapter 1, is a system that empowers you to mentally pair similar personality types together. These contacts could have a common denominator such as being parents with school-age children, being new entrepreneurs, or perhaps they are each looking for a person in one another's specific industry. As I noted in the previous chapter, it's very important to be as detailed as possible so you can refer correctly and productively.

Your first objective is to make connections that fill others' industry wheelhouses (see list of 84 industries in the Appendix). Your second objective is to make introductions from a cultural perspective. As long as you're doing the work of connecting people, you should try to help everyone create a more diverse network, and seek to have a diverse network yourself. Networking can benefit everyone from all walks of life. If your network only consists of people who look, sound, and act like you, or only believe the same things you do, then you are missing out on powerful connections. Whenever you can, try to make cross-cultural mirror matches. In the process, you'll make an impact and potentially bridge gaps between divided people.

I've made some absolutely fantastic personal and cultural mirror matches. The best mirror matches are those you connect who get along like two peas in a pod. I connected my entrepreneur friend Joy Williams and my graphic designer K Sonderegger. These are the commonalities I used to match them:

- Both have children.
- Both believe in Christ.
- Both lead from authenticity, they're very honest, and always do what's right.
- Both have been successful in network marketing.
- They have a similar sense of humor.
- They're interested in the same books.
- Their husbands have similar personalities.

Now the two of them are really good friends. They meet up frequently to eat meals and drink wine together; they can't thank me enough for connecting them.

Another mirror match that I'm particularly proud of was between my friend Jenny Beilsmith and my COO of Zero to 100™, Andrew Chao. These two think exactly the same! Here are some of the other criteria I used to match them:

- Both have two sons.
- Both are well-traveled.
- They like the same foods and hobbies.
- Both learn by "doing" rather than simply "reading."

Jenny and Andrew became such good friends, they're now in touch every other week. Jenny even went on to give Andrew free business coaching.

As mentioned previously, use your system to follow up with the introductions that were given and made, then in your next Hot Coffee meeting, cover which contacts were reached, meetings that were scheduled, and the experience each person had while contacting the introductions that the other provided. This process refines how and who you introduce moving forward based on the experience with the first group of introductions you gave to each other. It will also improve mirror matching within your network.

Networking Budget & ROI

Many people are hesitant to network because it's hard to track their return on investment. Tracking REAL-ationships that yield revenue is how you measure your gains with Zero to 100™ networking, but to know your overall ROI, you must be able to track the investment you make in *all* networking. Regardless of the networking method you use, you need a budget to support the growth of your business and have something against which to measure your ROI. Building a business is not easy and a plan is necessary to ensure you have a roadmap to reach all goals in a timely fashion while staying within your budget – particularly if you've started your business with borrowed money that needs to be paid back. **Most businesses include a marketing budget in their business plan, which is where you should allocate networking funds.**

Here are some questions to answer when forming a networking budget:

- How much should you budget?
- Where should you go to network?
- How many days a week do you plan to network?
- Does each event have a cost?
- Do you have to pay for your guests?
- Will you be networking during lunch only, earlier, or later in the day?
- What kind of costs are involved personally, like childcare or wardrobe?

Even if you're not sure about the exact numbers, do your best to estimate (which we'll cover in a moment). Your estimations can be reassessed quarterly until you get a solid feel for the costs. And, always overestimate by about 20% to make sure you're covered. One way to track spending is to log your networking endeavors and the outcomes in a journal or on a spreadsheet. Log each event, meeting, and – most importantly – what you spend. Journaling (or using a spreadsheet) is a wonderful tool to assist with tracking actual costs and budgeting. It provides an understanding of what does and doesn't work for you and your business. You should also note what does and doesn't go well during meetings so that moving forward you can incorporate what works to create success. Though I've been networking for years now, I am always adapting and tweaking my method because I can always be better.

The beauty of networking is that there are a massive variety of groups in your marketplace that are free to attend or cost a very minimal amount, like ribbon cuttings, some Chamber sponsored gatherings, and morning coffee groups or happy hours. These gatherings tend to be on a smaller scale, ranging from ten to forty people, which makes them perfect for in-depth connecting and minding your budget. Though there is not a weekly or monthly financial requirement, you might want to purchase a coffee or a bite to eat, so it's wise to include food and beverage in your budget.

Another great place to invest your marketing/networking budget is with a larger group that can provide more opportunities throughout the month to make connections. These may include 200-300 person monthly luncheons, seminars, or industry group meetings. Note that these recurring weekly, bi-weekly, or monthly events may require larger financial responsibility upfront or on a monthly or daily basis. However, you will certainly have more opportunities to meet other business owners and benefit from not only the event but the connections within the group.

So what items should you plan for when budgeting for networking?

1. Gas/Fuel – are you networking close to home/work or are you driving all over to Tour Guide network? Some months may be heavy, some lighter. Once you journal this, you'll get a better feel for your monthly average. If you track mileage instead of fuel, there are some great apps that track it and calculate it for you. If you do it yourself, keep a log in your car and write your starting odometer reading and the final reading when you are finished.

2. Auto Expenses – insurance, oil changes, tires, windshield wipers, roadside assistance memberships, other maintenance or supplies.

3. Supplies – digital business card, business cards/holder, brochures/handouts, paper/pens, and any giveaways.

4. Monthly, weekly, quarterly, yearly dues – do the dues include the monthly meal? Are there yearly dues on top of monthly? You can separate these in any way that makes sense to you. Want to have a yearly dues section and a weekly section? Maybe you break the yearly dues into a monthly amount and track monthly expenses only.

5. Weekly lunches – do you have to purchase lunch if an event is free? (It's courteous to purchase something out of respect and to support small businesses). Will this be in addition to your monthly dues?

6. Daily coffee – how often will you be meeting others, multiple meetings per day? Will you pay for your guests' coffee? I say pay for their coffee if it's within your means.

7. Attire – will you need a new wardrobe? Hair and nails? Do some events require more casual wear or business attire? Or perhaps evening wear? For example, if you buy a whole new wardrobe in January and add a few pieces in June, you may track it as such: $200 for clothes upfront + another $100 for some summer additions = $300 total, divided by 12 for a monthly cost of $25.

8. Sponsorships – these can be an occasional or yearly expense, like sponsoring a hole at a golf outing or an annual sponsorship for your local Chamber, etc.

9. Donations – very often you'll find nonprofit organizations raising money at Chamber luncheons. You will also notice many of your connections have a favorite charity that they support and may ask for donations toward that charity on occasion. This can really get away from you, as the feeling of obligation takes over. Set a monthly budget and stick to it. If you choose to allocate $25 a month to donations, when

you reach that, kindly tell your connection when they ask if you can donate, that you've met your monthly allotment, but you would be happy to help out next time. You can keep a list of who is connected with which nonprofit or cause and have that information for future donation planning.

10. Phone/Laptop/Other Internet Accessible Device – a quality WiFi-enabled device with reliable audio and video function is imperative for effective virtual networking and maintaining your network. You also need a reliable charger with your device.

11. A Reliable WiFi/Phone Service – free public WiFi isn't typically reliable enough to conduct meetings without interruptions, and the most stable WiFi connection is typically your home network (which is where most virtual networking is done). It's similarly important to have reliable phone service.

12. Video Platform – while you can use many video platforms for free, some video platform services offer expanded features for a small price.

13. Headphones/Earbuds – you need quality headphones or earbuds to optimize audio input and output during virtual networking. If your phone, laptop, or tablet doesn't have a good built-in microphone, budget for a listening device with a built-in microphone.

The following chart is a budgeting tool to help you get started. You can also find this on the website, www.zeroto100.io/start, and print it out.

Networking Expense	Average Monthly Cost	x12 = yearly cost
Fuel		
Travel Non-fuel expenses such as plane tickets, hotel stays, additional meals, etc.		
Networking Materials Business cards/holder, paper/pens, brochures/handouts and any give-aways		
Dues Memberships + weekly or monthly dues		
Meals/Coffee/Happy Hour		
Sponsorships		
Donations		
Attire		
Miscellaneous *List:*		
TOTAL		

Remember that networking itself is a business. Regardless of the type of networking, you choose, formulating a budget is essential to take your business to another level. Without a budget and the measurement of ROI from networking, there is no tool with which to measure your success. It is like traveling without knowing where you're going, how much it will cost to get there, how much it will cost while you're there, and how much money will be left to travel home. You simply could not do this without asking for trouble. Understand the networking budgeting process and plan accordingly to maximize your finances for the best results. Start now by researching your marketplace, then select the best options for your budget, needs, and wants. Building a new business can be taxing, but networking to grow with a mapped strategy will greatly benefit your growth and limit your financial and emotional stress.

Nothing creates confidence in your direction and goal attainment like a good plan.

> **Tip:** Budgeting documentation and regular tracking of costs will help you tremendously at tax time. Much of this can be written off as business expenses. And, you won't be scrambling to find this information and add it all up at the end of the year when it's time to consult your CPA.

Study Results: Participants' Financial Improvement

Networking can be considered a privileged activity. Many networking organizations charge a membership fee and let's be honest, there are costs involved to participate in networking events, such as fuel, drinks, and childcare. Virtual networking is also a privilege because it requires the networker to be able to afford a laptop and good internet service. However, participants of the study identified that implementing Zero to 100™ principles improved the financial investment of networking by 189%.

Bringing it Back to Coffee

Drinking and enjoying the most delicious hot coffee comes from the highest quality beans and budgeting for that ultimate result. Similarly, reaping the benefits of Hot Coffee networking means consistently contributing to others' networks and understanding the ROI of your networking endeavors by budgeting for them.

As you research groups, be sure to look into your local Chamber of Commerce and nonprofit groups like Kiwanis and the Lions Club. Here is a list of some specific national and international networking groups with membership dues and two podcasts (I do not endorse these for any reason other than they exist to help people connect!):

BNI-Business Networking International
https://www.bni.com/

Rockstar Connect
https://rockstarconnect.com/

Center Sphere – The Network;
www.CenterSphere.com

Master Networks
https://www.masternetworks.com/new-home-page

NTI-Networking Today International
https://networkingtodayintl.com/

Diverse Force
https://www.diverseforce.com/

Team Referral Networks
https://teamreferralnetwork.com/

PDP – Polka Dot Powerhouse
https://www.polkadotpowerhouse.com/

WEW – Women Empowering Women
www.wewnational.com

IWant2Network (Central London, England)
www.IWant2Network.com

Travis Chappell
Build Your Network
https://travischappell.com/podcast/

Robbie Samuels
On The Schmooze
www.OnTheSchmooze.com

If you sign up to visit any of these groups, there will be a section that asks, "How did you hear about us?" Please fill that in with Zero to 100™ as we are tracking how many of our readers go to these groups. Measuring results is the only way to gain understanding, just like budgeting and measuring ROI.

Join the Zero to 100™ Platform for help creating your networking budget: www.zeroto100.io/start

CHAPTER 9

Avoiding Bad Coffee
What to Do & What Not to Do in Networking Plus Common Pitfalls

Let's face it — we'll all sip a bad cup of coffee from time to time. Whether it's too bitter or watery, it will be a learning experience and you'll know what to watch for in the future. The same is true of networking. Just like bad coffee, there are indicators and red flags to watch out for. In this chapter, networking best practices are covered, as well as some of the common pitfalls.

Networking, when done with intention and a plan, is a tried-and-true way to promote and build your brand. It is also a cost-effective way of doing business. Most people already know that joining a networking group or attending an event is a wonderful way to get your name out there and meet others. But what if you are doing it all wrong? People spend hours each week or month at networking events, introducing themselves, and exchanging business cards, only to get mediocre results at best. When you attend these events collecting business cards and greeting as many people as possible, you end up missing those you were destined to meet and potentially miss your blessing. Even worse, you may miss the opportunity to bless another. As you network virtually, understand that virtual networking supports face-to-face events and vice versa. Virtual networking allows one to reach more people, and in-person meetings allow you to meet more hearts. While virtual networking is efficient, you can connect more genuinely in person — there's just something about the energy of meeting in person that allows REAL-ationships to blossom. If you can use both modes of networking, you can have a powerful network.

There are those rare occasions when you make that one connection that sets your business on fire — but honestly, how often does that happen? People network for years and go to countless groups and events without ever landing that one client who puts them on the map. Why does it take so long? Is it the events you choose or is it something you're doing? The reality is that the ideal client, customer, or referral partner has likely been right in front of you the entire time, you just didn't ask the right questions to unlock the opportunity.

I have compiled a list of networking tips from thousands of meetings that have proven to work for me in every networking environment. Let's start with the Do's of Networking. #1: *be on time!* The first and only impression you give others is whether you are on time for your events and meetings. Which goes hand-in-hand with how you show up mentally. You know the saying, "time is money"? I say, "thoughts are money." Because how you spend your time and how you show up to represent yourself is based on how you think. That will determine how you go about networking and connecting. This leads to #2: when you plan ahead and prepare to be on time (or a few minutes early), your entire demeanor will be professional and welcoming and that first impression, or even the fifth impression, will impress. Let's look at a complete list of the Do's and Don'ts and think about how many you already do or don't do and what you can change going forward.

"To be early is to be on time, to be on time is to be late, and to be late is to be forgotten."

— Elin Hilderbrand

Networking Do's:

- **First and foremost, be a little early for your event or meeting.** This allows you to get settled, calm your nerves, organize your papers/thoughts, and go into any meeting feeling confident. It's also a sign of respect to your guests when you're completely prepared, not rushing and adding stress to their day.
- Always give a firm nonverbal greeting, but lead with permission. There is a popular book called "The 5 Love Languages®: The Secret to Love That Lasts" by Gary Chapman first published in 1990 where he details the different love languages people use to show and receive love.[9] Well, there's also a networking language. Your networking language will naturally contain nonverbal cues, and prior to the pandemic I suggested a handshake or a hug, but now I recommend first asking the person you are greeting what they're comfortable with. Present them with the option to fist bump, elbow bump, foot tap, hug or shake hands, and only list the options that you, too, are comfortable with. Whatever greeting you decide to use, include good eye contact. Your greeting nonverbally communicates your personality and comfort level with a person. Each individual greeting means something. A firm handshake exudes confidence. A lighter handshake might mean you're more of an introvert. Are you a hugger? A side hug is cordial, but not comfortable. A crossbody hug is genuine. A bear hug says, "I've missed you." Maybe you elbow bump with new connections and fist bump or foot tap for those you've gotten to know. Whatever suits you, communicate nonverbally in a way that exemplifies your

personality and comfort level. Pick your networking language and stick with it. This helps those who network with you to learn what greeting to expect from you. You'll be your best self and most comfortable with your signature "hello" hand-shake/hug, and in closing when you nonverbally communicate, "Thank you, goodbye."

- **Make sure to have good eye contact the entire time you're speaking to someone.** It communicates a sense of trustworthiness and confidence while being comfortably engaged and focused (not glossed over).

- **Bring a pen, paper, tablet, computer, or even a recorder to take notes.** This shows that you're really absorbing what the other person is saying to you. Even if you're a weak note-taker, take notes anyway. I recommend note-taking on paper. It allows you to still engage and not be fooling with or distracted by technology. You can also opt to record your virtual meetings as long as you ask permission and explain why you want to record the meeting in advance.

- **Say the name of the person four or five times throughout the conversation when you first meet.** This helps solidify the person's name in your brain and also shows that you're personable and focused.

- **Turn your phone off or put it on vibrate.** Respect your guest and show that they are important and worth your time by not letting your phone disturb the meeting. Also, minimize all windows on your laptop if meeting virtually.

- **Canceling a meeting.** If you have to cancel a meeting, try to do it with plenty of time for the other person to rework their schedule (emergencies do happen, but don't make last-minute cancellations a habit) and leave it open-ended to reschedule.

Networking Don'ts:

- **Don't limit doing business with someone just because they're affiliated with your group.** Instead, do business with those in your group *and others* because you like them as people and trust and respect them.
- **Don't share your website in your elevator speech.** Nobody is going to write it down, it's too salesy, it's awkward, and it's on your business card. Instead, book a specific time to speak/meet with a person.
- **Don't wear your name tag.** First of all, wearing a name tag makes a person focus on trying to read your name tag rather than focusing on hearing you say your name. They're immediately less engaged and are more focused on the visual aid than listening to you. Second, wearing a name tag screams, "I want to sell to you." For the same reason, don't have your company logo or business card as your virtual background in video meetings. Virtual backgrounds are distracting in general and you want people to meet *you* the person, not you as the business.
- **Don't add someone to your email list or newsletter without their consent.** This could kill potential relationships because it tells people you're more interested in numbers than REAL-ationships. It's also spammy and an invasion of privacy.
- **Don't say you are too busy to meet with someone.** This tells the person you're either disrespectful with time, you're unorganized, your plate is full, or they're not that important. And you could miss out on business! Instead, say, "right now isn't a good time, when is a good time to get back with you?"
- **Don't overwhelm a person with a thousand different pieces of literature or promotional materials once you sit down.** Throwing up a stack of papers onto someone or sharing

a bunch of digital assets virtually during a Caffeinated Moment is overly sales-y and off-putting.

- **Don't bring additional people to your meeting unexpectedly.** It will hurt the opportunity to build a true relationship during the meeting.

I once met with a person who messed up our meeting time. Then, when we did meet, this individual brought a friend to our meeting and they both spent the time bombarding me with brochures and other marketing materials. It was not a good experience, and we weren't able to do any relationship-building.

Some of these Do's and Don'ts may seem trivial, but basic "connetiquette" matters (see Chapter 5). Even the little things matter when it comes to first impressions (after all — you really do only have one shot at this and that first impression never goes away). How you behave in meetings to showcase your best self, whether the first time or the fifth time, is very important to build powerful connections and maintain them.

Common Networking Pitfalls

Not everyone you meet with will come to the meeting with the intent to have Hot Coffee, so you should be prepared to encounter these two common networking pitfalls: Cold Coffee and Business Dating.

Cold Coffee

When two people come together for a Caffeinated Moment and seem to have all the chemistry in the world but nothing ever comes out of it, this is called a "cold cup of coffee." The other person may never follow up with the introduction or referral you provide and you may never see or hear from them again except in passing or on social media. This cold coffee experience can leave a bad taste in your mouth initially, but do not allow this to deter you from your networking objectives. When you first sip cold coffee, your face turns up, but you don't want to treat the person you're meeting with like this. Aim to be a great guide to a Caffeinated Moment and strive to be that first sip of warm, freshly brewed coffee for the person sitting across from you. When you keep the energy positive in all your meetings, you keep others from sipping that cold cup of coffee.

Please note that a "cold cup of coffee" may not understand how to have a Caffeinated Moment and it might be a good idea to schedule a second meeting. During this meeting, you can ask why this person didn't reach out to anyone you sent and may learn that they just have no idea how to follow up. And that's okay! This is a wonderful opportunity to share how to follow up, how to introduce yourself to others, and provide value, yet again, by demonstrating the key to networking is about relationships. Just remember – networking can be a very selfish sport; connecting is a team sport and sometimes it takes a good coach to get certain members of the team up to speed.

Tip: If you ever want to know how great your Caffeinated Moment was, call a person two weeks after you meet and ask him or her to explain what it is you do. If they can't properly explain what it is you do, then you need to schedule another meeting to apologize for not being clear, clarify what it is you do and have a better opportunity to receive good introductions or referrals.

Business Dating

BUSINESS DATING: WHERE TWO PEOPLE GET TOGETHER WITH NO INTENTION OF MAKING INTRODUCTIONS OR PASSING REFERRALS; YOU MIGHT AS WELL JUST SAY YOU WANTED TO TAKE A 1-HOUR LUNCH BREAK!

. -Jeff Ehrhardt- .

Some people network just to meet others, like the casual dating scene where a single person might go to dinner with someone. In this context, there are no intentions of having a second date or building REAL-ationships – so don't expect the "business date" to provide many introductions or referrals. A great way to keep business dating out of your meetings is to come to the table with tools in hand – pen, notepad, laptop – and ask intentional questions (Caffeinated Moment/"What's Your Story?" Questionnaire) that set the tone for a more productive meeting. Take it for what it's worth, but remember every person you spend time with is important and will have an impact on your life. **No one is ever a waste of your time, the only person's time you can waste is a person who lives an unplanned life.**

Everyone you meet is your future because you can truly learn something from everybody. You always have the potential to meet someone who may lead you to the one person who takes your business to the next level. More importantly, you may turn out to be exactly what your guest needs that day. Your positive energy, your outlook on life, or simply your desire to assist in your connection's success might just be what turns around their day, week, or entire business. Never take one meeting for granted. I'm sharing this to prepare you for all outcomes and **ensure that you know how to maintain your credibility in all situations by consistently providing value.**

Knowing how to recognize and navigate through meetings of either cold coffee or business dating will help you become a top-notch networker who knows how to productively communicate in any meeting.

Bringing it Back to Coffee

Understanding the not-so-great side of networking helps you identify and avoid potential bad experiences and remain professional in all situations – just like knowing the lengthy process of a delicious hot cup of coffee helps you avoid sipping a terrible cold cup of coffee. You now know how to create the best Hot Coffee experience every time.

The Zero to 100™ Experience

Networking is only worth the value you make of it. The intent of Zero to 100™ is to build meaningful connections through an actionable, measurable method and strategy. As you'll recall from the first chapter, here's the networking formula to success:

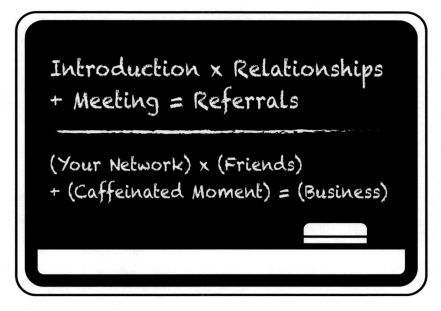

Introduction x Relationships + Meetings = Referrals
(Your Network) x (Friends) + (Caffeinated Moments) = (Business)

I hope this book has helped you learn the value of REAL-ationships in networking — it is at the core of this formula. Networking is an ever-changing game with one constant: relationships. There is always something you can learn from the person sitting (or virtually sitting) across from you in a meeting over coffee that helps you become a better networker. Everyone you meet has an impact on your future.

Networking is a marathon – not a sprint. Your objective should not be to sell to people – it should be to educate and empower people. Everything else you want out of networking will come as a byproduct of pursuing this objective.

1. Use the tools provided in this book to guide you in connecting with others.

2. Prioritize personality when making your introductions and referrals rather than industry.

3. To truly maximize what networking has to offer, your business needs to fill an industry wheelhouse.

4. Networking with people of different cultures, ethnicities, sexualities, abilities, and nationalities will expand your business in ways you never imagined while you actively do your part to create diversity in the business community.

5. If you're networking with intent and building REAL-ation-ships, you'll never have to justify the time or monetary investment.

I am not going to sugarcoat it – networking is hard work with very little return and a lot of outlay when you follow the status-quo. Using the Zero to 100™ networking methods to successfully build your business will make a lasting, measurable, emotional, spiritual, and financial impact.

What's Next?

The Zero to 100™ team is launching the Zero to 100™ Platform to help you put the book into practice and take your networking to the next level. This platform includes DISC and Motivator information, access to introductions and referrals that are always warm, a way to track the connections you make to understand your return on investment (ROI), and many other valuable tips and tools. As a member of this platform, you can also enhance your networking through Zero to 100™ Networking events with featured speakers and workshops based on the book.

To learn more about the Zero to 100™ Platform and events as well as receive updates, go to https://zeroto100.io/

Appendix

i. The Caffeinated Moment Form
Caffeinated Moment Form

This form is meant to be customized to your company/business to simplify the way you respond to a question like "What does your company do?"

As you may already know, my company is _____ **(name)** *and we have/are _____* **(background)**. *My company offers _____* **(product/service information)**. *So, you know about _____* **(competitor)**, *right? Well, this is how we are* **different**: *_____. Our* **market** *is _____. We typically* **deliver** *to our market by _____.*

Then give **background** about the company:

- When was the company started?
- How many customers/end users/clients do you have?
- The number of employees or type.
- Size of the company/how many locations.
- Is it privately owned, incorporated, partnership, etc.?
- Is the company debt free? Give revenue information (profitability/success of the business proves it's reputable).
- Where are you available to do business?
- Geography – where do you conduct business?
- Is your business an online model, offline model, or both? Does it have the capacity to run remotely?

Product: *General info about your product or service. If it makes sense, give a known example of what you do (maybe mention your competition), so your connection has a reference and knows how to compare you/share what you do with another.*

- Start by asking a general question like, "Are you familiar with what it is I do?" *(This tells you if your product/service applies to him or her, shows where their head is at, and which questions to ask.)*
- Ask questions/state facts about other products out on the market today to get a feel for their expectations/current understanding of your competition.
- Then, use their answers to adapt how you talk about your product or service to show how it is different and better suits this person's needs. This is your chance to create value in your product or service. State facts (nutritional value, statistics, etc).

Who is your market?:

- Residential, commercial, B2B, B2C, etc.
- Give specific industry(ies) and further specifics based on category. *(i.e. health and fitness industry-specific nutritionist, or whoever you are focusing on at that time.)*
- Additionally, state a location where you are trying to grow.

How to deliver your product/service into the market:

- Meetings over coffee/Caffeinated Moments.
- Through relationships/referrals.
- Free sample marketing through independent distributors.
- Cold calling.
- Retail store.
- Other:_____.

ii. Questions to Ask in a Virtual Meeting to Better Understand a Person's Personality

1. How do you like to spend your free time?
2. What was your dream job growing up?

3. If you had a chance for a "do-over" in life, what would you do differently?

4. What teacher in school made the most impact on you and why?

5. What is the craziest, most outrageous thing you want to achieve?

6. Would you rather live in the city, by the sea or in the woods? Why?

7. What characteristic do you most admire in others?

8. If you won the lottery, what would you do?

9. If you could travel anywhere, where would you go and why?

10. What is a skill you'd like to learn and why?

11. Which historical figure would you most like to be?

12. If you had to choose to live without one of your five senses, which one would you give up?

13. If you could take only five items with you to a deserted island, what would they be?

14. What is your best childhood memory?

15. If you could witness any event of the past, present, or future, what would it be?

16. What do you feel most proud of?

17. What was one of your most defining moments in life?

18. What is your ultimate goal in life?

19. Who is your biggest hero?

20. Tell me about your fears, what are you most afraid of?

iii. Joseph's Sample 60-Second Elevator Speech

"Good morning/afternoon/evening, I am Joseph Luckett with

Company ABC. We created the world's first nutritional, acid-free coffee. When you have regular coffee of any kind, it can cause acid reflux, jitters, shakes, and crashes, but one cup of our coffee contains the following nutrients per cup:

150 antioxidants, 200 vitamins and minerals, 800 times more vitamin B2 than Kiwi, three times more protein than peanut butter, three times more antioxidants than blueberries, and more. We focus on residential and commercial clients using our model called 'free sample marketing,' which allows the potential user to try before buying. This month, I would love an email introduction for the following three professions: lawyers, restaurant owners, and salon owners in St. Louis, Chicago, and New York. From an individual perspective, I would love to be introduced to John Smith, Owner of XYZ Business. Thank you, So-and-So, for inviting me to this group. My name is Joseph with Company ABC, bringing the treasures of the earth to the people of the world through one-of-a-kind coffee."

iv. What's Your Story? Questionnaire

If you would like to print this form to use, it may be found on the Zero to 100™ Platform, www.zeroto100.io/start

Name:

Date:

How long have you been networking?

Business Name:

Who introduced us?

Industry (Reference industry sheet):

1) Where are you from? *Their answer helps you relate better (i.e. if this person is from a small town, you may be able to talk about farming, community, etc.). People normally enjoy sharing about themselves.*

2) How many siblings? *They may be an only child or from a big family. In addition to helping you relate to your guest, this also gives you some insight into their upbringing. An only-child will act differently than someone with many siblings.*

3) Are you married, if so how long and how did you meet? *This is a chance for your connection to share about their personal life; gives you insight into family/spouse relationships, and provides an opportunity to relate to one another. Also, this may be a chance for a double dating opportunity with spouses to get to know them better.*

4) What does your spouse/partner do? *This can indicate how to make introductions or referrals for their spouse or partner.*

5) Do you have any kids, if so how many? *This is a great opportunity to relate as parents, sharing the joys and challenges of raising children.*

6) Do you have any pets? If so, what kind? Breed? *Many people who don't have children are passionate about their pets, and this question can give your connection a chance to open up and share more.*

7) Are you close to your siblings in terms of proximity and also relationship? *This gives insight into how this person may handle relationships, and if the person is family-oriented or not.*

8) Are you the first business owner or entrepreneur in your family? *This shows mindset – if this person is the first one in the family to own a business or if they inherited a family-owned business. Is it a struggle; is this person the oddball or black sheep of the family or is the family excited and supportive? It helps you relate and reinforces the family dynamic.*

9) What is the name of your business or the company you work for? How did you create the name if you own the business and why is it meaningful to you? *This tells you if your connection owns the business or is employed by a company.*

10) What do you do and why do you do it? *Storytime! This is an opportunity for you to get to know more about this person's business, their story, why and how they started the business. This is your time to sit and listen. Take notes on this person's story and be engaged with body language. If something is unclear, be sure to ask.*

11) Do you focus on residential or commercial? *This tells you what target market is the focus. Check all that are applicable*

- Residential
- Industrial
- Commercial
- B2C (Business to consumer)
- B2B (Business to business)
- Other: _____

12) How many employees do you have? *This should also be multiple choice and will tell you if you are personally able to service their needs in that area or if this person's needs are on a bigger scale than your business can provide. It also tells you if you can personally help or if there is some-one in your network who is more able to provide for/meet their needs. It also shows you what class of people you should connect him/her with. For example, if Johnny is a millionaire, match him with others of that capacity. There is a huge difference between a company that needs a $50,000 or $1,000,000 loan.*

- Employees
- Independent contractors

13) Do more of your sales come from... *Once you learn this it should help you direct him/her to the right source for business growth. Check all that are applicable.*

- **Word of mouth** (mostly based on reputation. People are more likely to share you with their friends based on how good their relationship is with you).
- **Internet** (e-commerce).
- **Networking** (events and meetings).

- **Social media** (online advertisements/posts on social media platforms).
- **Referrals** (one of your clients is using your product, has a good experience with it, and in mentioning it to friends, decides to give you their contact information. Word of mouth is more casual – you may or may not get contact info but your name is mentioned. Referrals, however, are where the friend agrees to share contact info with the intention of being contacted for that purpose).
- **Cold calling** (this is when you call people from a list where there is no relationship in the hopes of selling them on your service or product. This is probably one of the least effective ways to grow your business. I wouldn't advise it as one of your top 3 ways to promote yourself, especially if new to the world of business and networking.)
- **Advertising** (online, in print, TV, radio, etc.)

14) Are you a part of any Chambers of Commerce, if so, which one(s)? *This will tell you how your connection is building their business. It will also tell you if the person is satisfied in the Chamber and if not, it gives you a chance to invite this connection to your group and broaden their network. This is a good time to ask – if not a part of an organization already – whether they are open to joining one. Check all that are applicable.*

- **BNI** (Business Networking International)
- **NTI** (Networking Today International)
- **Master Networks**
- **Rockstar Connect**
- **Diverse Force**
- **TEAM Referral Network**
- **PDP Polka Dot Powerhouse**
- **WEW(Women Empowering Women)**
- **Mastermind**

- **CBL** (Christian Business Leaders)
- **IWant2Network** (Central London, England)
- **Self-Employed group**
- Other: _____

15) How long have you been networking? *(This tells you their current networking experience. It ensures you won't overwhelm or bore your guest. Also, ask what networking means to this person so you can tailor your meeting to their response.)*

16) Did you go to college and if so, where, and what did you major in? *(This is a way to relate to their experience. It can show you how much this person values or doesn't value education. Be careful not to place judgment or "put him/her in a box" based on the choice of school. In some places, this is a common practice, so be aware.)*

17) Is your business privately owned or publicly traded? *(This is more of an investing question. There may be stock options and this can potentially be an opportunity to talk further at a later time. One of your networking partners could benefit from this question as well.)*

18) Is your business franchised? *(It's an important question because there are parameters that must be followed when a business is franchised versus independently owned.)*

19) How long have you been in business? / How long have you been with your company? *(This tells where your guest is in terms of being an entrepreneur and it opens the door for you to ask how big their network is.)*

20) Do you have a source of residual income coming into your household currently, and if so which company are you with? *(This question is optional– it's meant for people in the profession of network marketing. It tells you if this person is already in/comfortable with the network marketing industry and for you to potentially make recommendations.)*

21) Do you like to read or work on personal growth and if so, what is your preferred source? *(Check one or more of the following that* *applies)* **Also, what is your favorite genre?** *(This tells you if this person is working on themself and if interested in learning/improving/growing.)*

- Hardback/softcover books
- Audibles
- Kindle
- Ebooks
- Articles
- Podcasts
- Youtubers
- Conference/seminars

Genre? _____

22) Do you like movies or documentaries, and if so what genre? *(Make recommendations if you have any.)*

23) What social media platforms are you on? *(This can give you a chance to introduce him/her to something new. Check all that apply.)*

- Facebook
- Linkedin
- Alignable
- Nextdoor
- Shapr
- Instagram
- Pinterest
- Twitter
- Snapchat
- YouTube
- Other

24) Can I add you to my social media platforms? *(Make sure you get their business card if you don't already have it. You want to stay connected. After all, the goal here is to build your audience.)*

- Yes
- No

25) Would you be willing to leave a review on my Facebook/ Linkedin/other, sharing something that I taught you? Perhaps something that helped you personally or professionally? *(Use this as a rating system to help you gauge how much value you added (or did not add) to the meeting. It then allows you to continually build your business according to what the market is saying, which allows eternal growth. Additionally, this is a way to keep yourself from being self-serving because you cannot genuinely help people and have an ego.)*

26) Who or What would be a great introduction for you? Please be industry-specific. *(List names for all that apply so you know how to properly introduce this person to the appropriate connections.)*

Note: You, driving the meeting, fill in the blanks with your connections in whatever category fits their needs. For example, they say "realtors," so you list the realtors in your network who would be a good fit. It is important to remember, you will have him/her fill out this same form later, once you get to this part of the meeting. You are going to have him/her repeat the same process for you. This means your connection will list people they know personally to connect with you on the topic(s) you select. The point of going through this process in your meeting is to create an action of actually connecting people with others instead of just talking about it.

27) How many Introductions can you handle per month? *(You ask this so you can be careful not to overwhelm your connection, but keep their schedule filled. Circle what applies.)*

    A) 1-5

    B) 6-10

    C) 11-15

    D) 16-20

    E) Other, please put a specific number ____.

28) Who would be a great referral for you? *(Ask this to properly fulfill the number of referrals needed while providing the best quality referrals.)*

29) How would you like to receive these warm introductions? *(You are just honoring their preferences on how to be contacted. Check all that apply.)*

- Text
- Facebook Messenger
- Email
- LinkedIn
- Instagram DM
- Phone call
- Other

v. Industry Wheelhouse

It is important to continue to add more of the staple industries to your contact list and never really stop. Have 10 chiropractors? 25 insurance agents? That's great! Why?

When it comes to many industries, the failure rate is very high. If you have multiples in your wheelhouse to refer/introduce, you won't lose out. According to BizMiner, of the 1,021,350 general contractors and operative builders, heavy construction contractors, and special trade contractors operating in 2014, only 722,281 were still in business in 2016. This is a 29.3% failure rate. Other industry failure rates to know:

Real estate agents: 87% failure rate; only 13% make it.

Insurance agents: 90% fail; only 10% make it.

Financial advisors: 88% fail; only 12% make it.

Here is the Industry Wheelhouse List of 84 industries. This is not meant to be exhaustive but based on my experiences.

Personal Care	Marketing & Branding	Family Services	Real Estate Services
Chiropractor:	Business Consultant:	Day Care:	Mortgage Broker:
Cosmetics & Skin Care:	Graphic Designer:	Veterinarian:	Real Estate Agent (Residential):

Personal Care	Marketing & Branding	Family Services	Real Estate Services
Personal Trainer:	Promotional Products:	Funeral Planning:	Real Estate Agent (Commercial):
Nutritional Products:	Website Design:	Assisted Living:	Title Company:

Personal Care	Marketing & Branding	Family Services	Real Estate Services
Massage Therapist:	Printer:	Pet Grooming/Boarding:	Appraiser/Inspector:
Dentist:	Bulk Mailing:	Educational Products:	Blinds/Window Treatments:

Personal Care	Marketing & Branding	Family Services	Real Estate Services
Spa/Salon:	Sign Shop:	Nursing Home:	Auctioneer:
Dietician or Nutritionist:	Trade Show Coordinator:	Automotive Sales:	Moving Company:

Personal Care	Marketing & Branding	Family Services	Real Estate Services
Jeweler:	Business/Magazine Publications:	Automotive Repair:	Security Systems:
Optometrist:	Marketing Consultant:	Dry Cleaning/Laundry:	Interior Decorator:

Personal Care	Marketing & Branding	Family Services	Real Estate Services
Therapist (general):	Life Coach:	Education/Tutor:	Other:

Events/ Weddings	Business Support	Insurance/ Financial	Contractors
Event Planner:	Accountant/CPA:	Accountant/CPA:	HVAC Heating & Cooling:

Events/ Weddings	Business Support	Insurance/ Financial	Contractors
Florist:	Attorney- General/Business Law:	Insurance- Long Term Care:	Carpeting/Flooring:
Gift Baskets:	ISP:	Insurance Home & Auto	Carpet Cleaning:

Events/ Weddings	Business Support	Insurance/ Financial	Contractors
Photographer:	Business/Marketing Consultant:	Insurance–Life & Health:	Residential/Commercial Cleaning:
Videographer:	Computer Consultant:	Insurance–Commercial	Landscaping:

Events/ Weddings	Business Support	Insurance/ Financial	Contractors
Travel Agent:	Office Equipment:	Insurance– Supplemental:	Handyman:
Hair Stylist:	Telecommunication Systems:	Employee Benefits:	General Contractor:

Events/ Weddings	Business Support	Insurance/ Financial	Contractors
Caterer:	Payroll Service:	Personal Banking:	Roofing:
Limousine Service:	Staffing Agency:	Financial Planning:	Siding/Windows:

Events/ Weddings	Business Support	Insurance/ Financial	Contractors
Formal Apparel:	Network Administrator:	Attorney- Family Law:	Electrician:
DJ:	Office Supplies:	Attorney- Estate Planning:	Plumber:

Events/ Weddings	Business Support	Insurance/ Financial	Contractors
Haberdashers/Pro Clothiers:	Lawyer:	Financial Advisor:	Other:

vi. Email Introduction Template

Subject Line: ABC Meet XYZ, XYZ meet ABC

ABC, XYZ is a _____. *(Short Intro: Say something nice about XYZ, share important accolades and achievements, explain how they're doing well and love helping people, plus any other important background information relevant to this introduction. This is essentially a short bio on XYZ and the reason that XYZ will be a good pairing for ABC).*
(Expanded Intro: Include a hobby or sport this person is interested in, a favorite food, preferred genre of books or movies, and if this person is a family person).

XYZ, ABC is _____. *(Repeat the above process in parenthesis)*
ABC, go ahead and start scheduling meetings over coffee with XYZ (and other individuals listed.)
<u>ABC Contact Info</u>
Name, phone, email
All their social media links (Facebook, Instagram, LinkedIn, Twitter, Alignable, etc.)
<u>XYZ Contact Info</u>
Name, phone, email
All their social media links (Facebook, Instagram, LinkedIn, Twitter, Alignable, etc.)
Sincerely,
Your signature
Tagline

vii. National and international networking groups for your reference:

BNI – Business Network International
https://www.bni.com/

WNA – Women's Network Australia
https://www.womensnetwork.com.au/

Rockstar Connect
https://rockstarconnect.com/

Center Sphere – The Network
www.CenterSphere.com

Master Networks
https://www.masternetworks.com/new-home-page

NTI – Networking Today International
https://networkingtodayintl.com/

Diverse Force
https://www.diverseforce.com/

Team Referral Networks
https://teamreferralnetwork.com/

PDP – Polka Dot Powerhouse
https://www.polkadotpowerhouse.com/

WEW – Women Empowering Women
http://www.wewnational.com

IWant2Network (Central London, England)
www.IWant2Network.com

Travis Chappell – Build Your Network
https://travischappell.com/podcast/

Robbie Samuels – On The Schmooze
www.OnTheSchmooze.com

Glossary

51/49 Rule: Always supply 51% of the value in your networking efforts.

Business Dating: When two people get together with no intention of making introductions or passing referrals – you might as well just take a one-hour lunch break.

B2B: Business-to-business transactions; a business that sells to other businesses.

B2C: Business-to-consumer transactions; a business that sells directly to consumers.

Caffeinated Moment: The one-to-one meeting where you get to know your connection.

Caffeinated Moment Form: A form used to easily answer questions about your company and who you are looking for.

Cold Coffee: When two people have a meeting at a coffee shop with all the chemistry in the world and nothing ever comes of it, then you either see them in passing or never again.

Coffee Maintenance: Genuine touchpoints with referral partners in between your meetings to add value to your relationship (birthdays, holidays, throw an event, calling, texting, emails). Not canned responses like the Facebook birthday post suggestions.

Coffee Shop Experience: Treat every person as a guest and make him or her feel comfortable.

Connetiquette: Showing proper respect for the people you meet with.

Cultural Wheelhouse: Networking with people of different cultures, ethnicities, sexualities, abilities, and nationalities to expand your business while you actively do your part to create diversity in the business community.

DISC: A behavior model developed by William Marston, Ph.D., that addresses the way people respond to problems and challenges (D), people and contacts (I), pace and consistency (S), and procedures and constraints (C). Your specific DISC profile is a blend of the four behaviors.

Effective Networking: When you learn about a person both personally and professionally and have their best interest at heart 100% of the time, and the other person reciprocates. Once that has been accomplished, you should be able to look into your database or network and start making connections.

Elevator Speech: Your pre-prepared commercial where you share your work/company, your competition, and why you are different or unique. Depending on the length, it may include who your target market is and how you are delivering your product or service to that market.

F.O.R.M.: A group of topics (Family/Friends, Occupation, Recreation, Message) that resonate universally with anyone you network with because they comfortably guide you in and out of conversations.

Highjacking: When you're meeting someone in a coffee shop and a person comes over to your booth to be introduced to your guest. This person either slides in the booth nearby or starts asking questions that could be saved for a separate meeting.

Hot Coffee Networking: Consistently contributing to each other's networks and reaping an ROI from your networking endeavors.

Hybrid Networking: A combination of both face-to-face networking and virtual networking.

Industry Wheelhouse: A list of 84 different industries to try to supply to your connections in networking.

Introduction: When two people are introduced to one another through a friend or mutual acquaintance. There is an established level of trust where both parties are comfortable opening their network and bringing people to the table that can benefit each other's revenue line, network, or both.

Leads: Leads are cold contacts. They are typically just a person's name, business, and contact information. No personal introduction and no prior relationship.

Meetings Over Coffee: Networking meetings with one simple purpose: for you to get to know each other.

Mirror Matching: A system that empowers you to pair similar personality types together.

Motivators: Based on the work of Eduard Spranger, Ph.D., the six motivators address what drives or motivates people to do what they do.

Networking: Meeting people, sharing what you both do, and finding ways to help one another.

Networking Budget: The funds that are allocated toward all networking expenses, which may be included in a marketing budget. Specific expenses could include gas, coffee, meals, monthly/yearly/quarterly dues, vehicle maintenance, wardrobe, self-development (books, audiobooks, movies, etc.), and time.

Networking Meeting: When a community of business owners, from rookies to veterans, gather in one location to casually learn about one another, shake hands, and socialize.

Networking Tree: A way to track who you've been introduced to.

Pain Points: A specific problem that prospective customers are experiencing.

Red Flag: An industry that is not a good use of your time.

Referrals: Connections to people who are already warmly interested in your product or service – people who are likely to feed your business revenue.

Referral Partners: Where two strangers are warmly introduced to each other through mutual friends/acquaintances with the sole purpose of learning about each other personally and professionally, with a result of impacting each other's revenue line, network, or both in a marathon of growing a long-lasting relationship.

Stack Days: When you schedule all your meetings in one day at the same location, a half-hour to one hour apart, to be most efficient with your time.

Tour Guide: Someone who acts as your guide to a new network in a new place (city, state, country) and introduces you to people in that network.

Tour Guide Reciprocity: When tour guides exchange introductions in each others' communities and other parts of the country or world.

Virtual Networking: Networking meetings that take place over a video platform or the phone.

References

1. Schmidt, D. (2019). [The study of the relationship between the Zero to 100™ strategies and networking benefits in a real-world trial]. Unpublished raw data. *(RESULTS OF THE Zero to 100™ DATA STUDY)*

2. *Ganoderma Coffee & Tea: Organic Ganoderma Lucidum.* Organo Gold. (2020, July 2). https://www.organogold.com/en/. *(Introduction: Planting the Coffee Seed – Who is Joseph Luckett?)*

3. Thomson Reuters. (2018, March 17). *Americans are drinking a daily cup of coffee at the highest level in six years: survey.* Reuters. https://www.reuters.com/article/us-coffee-conference-survey/americans-are-drinking-a-daily-cup-of-coffee-at-the-highest-level-in-six-years-survey-idUSKCN1GT0KU. *(Chapter 1: Growing the Coffee Cherry – What is Networking?)*

4. Marston, W. M. (1928). *Emotions of Normal People.* London: K. Paul, Trench, Trubner & Co. Ltd.; New York: Harcourt, Brace, and Co., 1928. *(Chapter 2: Harvesting the Coffee Cherry to Get the Best Bean – Using DISC & Motivators to Understand Networking)*

5. TTI Success Insights is an industry-leading assessment provider based in Scottsdale, AZ. Their research-based, validated assessment and coaching tools enable organizations to meet their talent management needs effectively. The TTI SI network spans over 58 countries and works to bring people-focused solutions to teams across the world by revealing human potential. *(Chapter 2: Harvesting the Coffee*

Cherry to Get the Best Bean – Using DISC & Motivators to Understand Networking)

6. Pollard, M., & Lewis, D. B. (2021). *The Introvert's Edge to Networking: Work the Room. Leverage Social Media. Develop Powerful Connections.* HarperCollins Leadership, an imprint of HarperCollins Focus LLC. *(Chapter 3: Sorting & Pulping the Cherry – Identifying Types of Networkers & Networking Groups)*

7. Cowsert, L. (2018). *Character: Lessons Learned from a Character ... About Having Character.* Westcor Publishing, LLC. *(Chapter 3: Sorting & Pulping the Cherry – Identifying Types of Networkers & Networking Groups)*

8. *Business Network International: Business Networking.* BNI. (2021, January 9). https://www.bni.com/. *(Chapter 3: Sorting & Pulping the Cherry – Identifying Types of Networkers & Networking Groups)*

9. Chapman, G. D., & Green, J. (2017). *The 5 Love Languages: The Secret to Love That Lasts.* Northfield Publishing. *(Chapter 9: Avoiding Bad Coffee – What to Do & What Not to Do in Networking Plus Common Pitfalls)*

FURTHER ACKNOWLEDGMENTS

Thank you to my beta readers:

Angela Warfield, Lindsay Rapp, and many of my invaluable board members.

Thank you to all the people who inspired my love for education, including:

Keacha Bradley, Tara Matthews, Cierra Caldwell.

Thank you to all of you who showed me the importance of transparent counsel, including:

Rayleen, Kay, and Kerry.

Thank you to all of you who showed me the importance of personal style, including:

Roderick, Harold, Nick, and Lamont.

Thank you to Anya Overmann who is not only a Board Member but the content writer that helped me incredibly. You listened to me tell my story, spent over 150 hours writing and editing, and fact-checked everything to ensure we come out of the gate 10 feet tall! I cannot thank you enough and I look forward to making a lot of noise across the globe with your game-changing content writing!

Thank you to Cindy Wiltse of Cindy's Photo Impressions and Kim Eichelberger of Eichelberger Photography for all you have done for our Advisory Board, snapping all the headshots to ensure we have the same tone across the company!

Thank you to Jessica Schroer, Founder & CEO of the Hummingbird Group LLC for literally pulling our entire company together, ensuring that we will have unprecedented success! I've never seen anyone put systems and processes together like you. I'm totally stoked to bring such a unique concept and company across the globe and honored to have you on my Advisory Board!

Thank you to K. Sonderegger, owner of Made You Look Design and Marketing, for the awesome design of the Zero to 100™ logo, book cover, and internal graphics. You have been immensely important in getting the "feel" of our mission just right and our entire team is grateful for your creativity and beautiful spirit.

Thank you to one of my initial book editors, Kristin D. Sadler. Kristin was instrumental in getting the voice of the book just right and helping the early version of the manuscript come together, which paved the way for any newly written chapters and additions to be written/edited accordingly. Kristin, we are uber-grateful – all of the folks who will read this, the entire board, and my wife and I.

Thank you to the people who have inspired me to be a better Christian by always keeping me grounded, keeping people first, always living the highest standard of character, and never being judgmental:

Casaundra Joliff, Samantha Carter, Scott Nyberg, Pam and Kevin French, Joy Bryant, Benjamin Golley, Mike McCann, Bruce Sheridan, John Thrower, Michael Plunkett, Mark Coppersmith, Christopher Vassel, Tony Holt, Alicia Saint Ives, Christy Sparks, and many more.

About the Authors

Carol Luckett and her husband Joseph are co-founders of Zero to 100™, an inclusive networking movement that operates on a global scale.

After Joseph was first exposed to networking and felt as though he wasn't welcome, he made it his mission to make everyone he met feel special and lend a helping hand anywhere he went. As an "ambivert" (a combination of an *extrovert* and an *introvert*), Joseph loves networking and sees the potential in everyone he meets. As he says, "everyone you meet is your future."

Carol's experience with networking was quite different. She was first exposed when she was working as a financial adviser and then as the General Manager of a restaurant she was promoting. She felt welcomed in networking but sensed that many people had self-serving agendas, which caused her to retreat into her *introversion*.

Although they had very different experiences, they shared in the belief that business networking lacks inclusivity, universal, and efficient processes.

Joseph's unique twist to networking and desire to help everyone he met birthed the book *Zero to 100: The Gold Standard of Global Networking* and the beginning of the Zero to 100™ movement.

Carol and Joseph have an amazing relationship and find joy in working together with their humor for one another's quirks.

When this dynamic duo isn't working towards their goals, you can find them spending time with their closest friends enjoying the outdoors or at home cooking for everyone.